Population Health and Vulnerable Populations

Cognella Series on
Public and Community Health Nursing

Population Health and Vulnerable Populations

Anita Finkelman, MSN, RN

SAN DIEGO

Bassim Hamadeh, CEO and Publisher
Amanda Martin, Publisher
Amy Smith, Senior Project Editor
Jeanine Rees, Production Editor
Jess Estrella, Senior Graphic Designer
Kylie Bartolome, Licensing Associate
Natalie Piccotti, Director of Marketing
Kassie Graves, Vice President of Editorial
Jamie Giganti, Director of Academic Publishing

This book is designed to provide educational information and motivation to our readers. It is sold with the understanding that the publisher is not engaged to render any type of psychological, legal, diet, health, exercise or any other kind of professional advice. The content of each chapter or reading is the sole expression and opinion of its author, and not necessarily that of the publisher. No warranties or guarantees are expressed or implied by the publisher's choice to include any of the content in this volume. Neither the publisher nor the individual author(s) shall be liable for any physical, psychological, emotional, financial, or commercial damages, including, but not limited to, special, incidental, consequential or other damages. Our views and rights are the same: You are responsible for your own choices, actions, and results and for seeking relevant topical advice from trained professionals.

3970 Sorrento Valley Blvd., Ste. 500, San Diego, CA 92121

This project is dedicated to all the students who have taught me during my years of professional practice in clinical and academic settings. I also recognize the nurses who have provided care daily during a difficult time of a pandemic, treating all equally in all settings and communities, and hold special thoughts for those nurses who experienced illness and lost their lives as they worked to improve the health of their communities.

Contents

ACTIVE LEARNING

This book has interactive activities available to complement your reading.

Your instructor may have customized the selection of activities available for your unique course. Please check with your professor to verify whether your class will access this content through the Cognella Active Learning portal (http://active.cognella.com) or through your home learning management system.

Preface

D ue to our experience with the COVID-19 pandemic, nurses have encountered many new challenges and questioned the quality of past healthcare delivery and education. This has impacted and will continue to affect all aspects of healthcare delivery globally, including nursing. This content focuses on improving public and community health and emphasizes the need for the nursing profession and the healthcare delivery system to recognize that we must do more to make public and community health an integral part of healthcare delivery. Nursing students are eager to "get into *real* nursing" in the hospital; however, after our experiences with COVID-19, we now should be more aware that public and community health is critical for the health of individuals, families, populations, communities, and individual countries as well as globally and affects all aspects of life. We also now have a greater recognition that this is not a simple area of healthcare, which has long been a common view. Public and community health is influenced by equity and justice, culture, policies, governments, laws, ethics, and economics, among other factors. In addition, health information changes quickly, which requires nurses to be aware of changes and new information and then integrate the information into their public and community health practice. This is not easy to accomplish, and it is complex due to the need to consider a broad variety of factors—the social determinants of health (SDOH). Population health and vulnerable populations have an impact on the overall health status of communities and countries. This requires attention to health equity and recognition that we have serious disparities in health delivery and outcomes that must be addressed in all healthcare settings. The nursing profession has acknowledged these issues through recent revisions of nursing education standards and its ethics, including statements about racism, discrimination, health equity, and disparities and strategies to improve population health. We need more nursing student experiences in a variety of healthcare settings, in addition to acute care, to prepare a nursing workforce that can also practice effectively in public and community health. Major reports from experts recognize that the need for change must be addressed. *The Future of Nursing 2020–2030: Charting a Path to Achieving Health Equity* (National Academy of Medicine, 2021), the third report in a series on the future of nursing, indicates that nursing education must consider and integrate content and clinical experiences that address SDOH, health equity, and population health, which are not currently integrated in curricula. Students need clinical experiences with various people, diverse life experiences, and cultural values. This guide focuses on population health and vulnerable populations in healthcare delivery, which are important to the nation's health.

Acknowledgments

I thank my family for their support of my writing and professional endeavors over many years: Fred, Shoshannah, Deborah, and especially my grandson, Matanel Yizhar, who teaches me daily that learning is constant as well as caring. Thank you to Amanda Martin, a long-time publishing colleague who reached out to me to reconnect to develop this project. The Cognella team cannot be praised enough for their professionalism and creativity: Amy Smith for directing editing guidance and keeping me on track; Dani Grandsher, Haley Brown, and all the others who helped with the development of methods supporting creative student engagement in learning and effective faculty resources; Jeanine Rees for guiding production; Jess Estrella for creative covers; Natalie Piccotti, who leads the marketing initiative; and so many others who have helped on this project behind the scenes.

Population Health and Vulnerable Populations

Learning Outcomes

1. Integrate population health into nursing practice in public and community health to decrease health disparities.

2. Assess the key health needs of major vulnerable populations and their relationship to public and community health, social determinants of health, health equity, and disparities.

3. Examine examples of key population health policies, programs, and interventions.

4. Apply nursing roles and interventions to the needs of vulnerable populations in the community and improve population health.

5. Formulate a summary statement highlighting key points about population health and vulnerable populations and nursing care in the community to ensure effective public and community health and decrease health disparities.

Key Terms

BIPOC (Black, Indigenous, and People of Color)
Case management
Disease prevention
Diversity
Health literacy
Health disparities

Health equity
Health promotion
Misinformation
Population health
Population health management
Registry

Social determinants of health (SDOH)
Social vulnerability
Surveillance
Triple Aim
STEEEP®
Vulnerable populations

Introduction: Population Health and Vulnerable Populations

The first section of this guide examines population health and its connection to public and community health. There are several perspectives of population health. This content presents information about frameworks, concepts, and measurement related to population health and other aspects of this area of healthcare. **Population health** is "the health outcome of a group of individuals, including the distribution of such outcomes within the group" (Kindig & Stoddart, 2003, p. 367). This perspective of health includes health outcomes but also patterns of health determinants and related policies and interventions. Identified populations share clinical conditions and may live in the same geographic area (e.g., a community [neighborhood, town, city], county, or state). Within these locations there is diversity; however, even in communities with diverse populations some policies and infrastructure are shared by all in the community for example, social services, law enforcement, transportation. The overarching healthcare goal is healthy people in healthy communities.

Healthcare delivery tends to emphasize acute care and often does not actively engage in ensuring healthcare for all. Public and community health is a critical part of the healthcare delivery system and should be integrated with acute care and vice versa. The recent global pandemic has further highlighted this concern. The content in this guide emphasizes the public and community health perspective in providing population healthcare to vulnerable populations. Nurses are involved in this aspect of healthcare delivery; however, there must be more nursing involvement—in providing care, planning programs to meet needs, participating in policy development and implementation, working with communities, and advocating for population health. In addition to examining key population health frameworks and concepts, vulnerable populations and their health needs are described in this text. The content examines health policies, interventions, and programs to address the population health needs and discusses nurses' roles and responsibilities in this area of healthcare delivery. More attention is now being given to BIPOC (Black, Indigenous, People of Color) populations and the need to ensure health equity and decrease disparities in healthcare services by guaranteeing that policies and health reimbursement support health equity, inclusion healthcare profession education, and increasing workforce diversity.

A survey of healthcare leaders in multiple states from the states' most populous cities provides information about concerns this important group has about healthcare. They were also asked what they were doing about the problems (Gooch et al., 2022). The survey was conducted during the COVID-19 pandemic. COVID-19 presented many challenges to the healthcare system, but the leaders also noted other problems. The survey indicated that population health, with examples identified such as mental health, obesity, and substance use disorders (SUD), was a major concern. Other problems identified were social isolation, particularly related to COVID-19, and **social determinants of health** (SDOH), such as food insecurity. It is significant that hospital leaders recognize the importance of equitable access and have now identified improvement as a main priority for their healthcare organizations. This survey indicates that the key topics in healthcare recognized by healthcare organization leaders include the impact of COVID-19, population health, vulnerable populations, and health equity and disparities. Nurses must assume leadership in population health, but first, they need knowledge about these areas of health and healthcare delivery, as attaining an understanding of these issues is critical to effective nursing practice.

Population Health and Population Health Management in Public and Community Health

This section introduces frameworks and concepts and examines the importance of population health and population health management, including measurement. Population health is integral to effective public and community health.

Frameworks and Key Concepts

The American Hospital Association (AHA) describes a population health framework that emphasizes health and equity and identifies the key focus areas as integrated care models, chronic/complex care, and community partnerships (AHA, 2020). The goals are population health improvement and community well-being. This framework agrees with other perspectives of population health management and the need for greater understanding of populations, leadership, advocacy, change, expansion of knowledge and sharing (e.g., using evidence-based practice), and measurement and monitoring of needs and outcomes. The AHA framework recognizes commitment to access, health, innovation, and affordability (AHA, 2022). This all relates to the **Triple Aim**, the goals of which are to "improve the individual experience of care, improve the health of populations, and reduce the per capita costs of care for populations. Health equity is not a fourth aim, but rather an element of all three components of the Triple Aim. The Triple Aim will not be achieved until it is achieved for all" (Wyatt et al., 2016).

Review the graphic of the AHA Population Health Framework. Write a brief summary describing the framework.
Website: https://www.aha.org/center/population-health-fundamentals

Population health focuses on the health status and outcomes for a group of people (i.e., population) and not on individual needs and health. Although the entire healthcare delivery system should be engaged in meeting the needs of all populations, public and community health services are particularly involved in this aspect of health. The most effective population health services and outcomes, however, are based on a collaborative acute care and public and community health partnership—as demonstrated in the AHA population health framework, for example, which emphasizes collaboration. This may seem strange that an organization that mostly represents acute care organizations (although AHA is also engaged in some aspects of community health) recognizes the need to collaborate with all types of healthcare services and not focus only on acute care. The goal is the health of all populations in a community, which requires more than solely acute care services.

There are many factors that impact population health, including social, economic, environmental, and individual behavioral and genetic traits (National Association of Community Health Centers [NACHC], 2016). Population health is also concerned with **health equity**, which is:

> ... when all members of society enjoy a fair and just opportunity to be as healthy as possible. Public health policies and programs centered around the specific needs of communities can promote health equity. The U.S. Department of Health and Human Services (HHS) and its agencies such as the Centers for Disease Control and Prevention (CDC) are committed to understanding and appropriately addressing the needs of all populations, according to specific cultural, linguistic, and environmental factors. By ensuring health equity is integrated across all public health efforts, all communities will be stronger, safer, healthier, and more resilient. (HHS, CDC, 2022a)

Population health is a major focus of public health. The CDC acknowledges the following definition for public health that was first used in 1920 and continues to be relevant today: "The science and art of preventing disease, prolonging life, and promoting health through the organized efforts and informed choices of society, organizations, public and private communities, and individuals" (HHS, CDC, 2021a; Wilson, 1920).

The healthcare system should be concerned with individual health equity, but population health looks at health equity from the perspective of the population rather than just focusing on individuals. It is concerned with improving health equity and clinical health outcomes for a population. Accomplishing this important goal requires interprofessional teamwork and collaboration and includes the following activities (National Committee for Quality Assurance [NCQA], Healthcare Effectiveness Data and Information Set [HEDIS], 2019).

- **Population analysis:** Data collection and analysis to better understand risks, needs, and outcomes for specific populations
- **Clinical integration:** Healthcare services based on population needs, including immunizations, health screenings, and care focused on specific needs, such as hypertension and diabetes
- **Care management/coordination:** Team-based, patient-centered care focused on population health needs and management of health
- **Patient engagement:** Active support of population (i.e., individuals, families, groups) involvement in healthcare decision-making, planning, implementation, and evaluation of healthcare
- **Telehealth integration:** Use of technology to provide, monitor, and document health as well as services; includes population involvement for both individuals and groups
- **Claims management:** Process of identifying and ensuring requirement of payment for services

Public health focuses on protecting and improving the health of communities by developing and using effective policies, providing health education, and engaging the public in health decisions. Public health activities are related to health promotion, surveillance, monitoring, epidemic assessment and response, disease prevention, communication, risk management, and research. The CDC is an HHS agency that focuses on public health activities, particularly outreach and research for disease detection and injury prevention. During the COVID-19 pandemic, the CDC frequently shared information and guidelines with the public through the media (television, radio, print, Internet). *Public health* is a term that is used more by government and policymakers, whereas the term *community health* tends to apply more to specific geographic areas, such as cities and counties. **Appendix A** provides more information about public health and its functions and essential services.

Before examining population health, it is important to recognize that *population health* can be a confusing term and that universally accepted definitions are not yet available. Population health includes consideration of health outcomes for a population, and population health management, which focuses on what is done to ensure health for a population and may also be referred to as *population medicine*. The following offers a comparison of these terms:

> Population health, then, is informed by population medicine; the actions taken create the results that population health analysts and experts take into account when reporting on and studying the health of a population. The two terms also different in one other way; while population health can mean global health or a particular demographic, population medicine targets a total population, such as the population of a nation. (Kindig & Stoddart, 2003, p. 267)

Another description notes that population health is "the design, delivery, coordination, and payment of high-quality health care services to manage the Triple Aim for a population using the best resources we have available to us within the health care system" (Lewis, 2014).

Population Health Management

The **population health management** process is applied by healthcare providers, policymakers, and services and includes the following steps:

- Define the focus population.
- Identify core gaps in health and care.
- Stratify risks for the population, including consideration of SDOH.
- Develop a plan identifying interventions and timeline.
- Engage providers and patients in the process.
- Manage care as needed.
- Track and evaluate outcomes, using analysis results to improve.

The process includes the same steps as the nursing process (i.e., assess, diagnose, plan, implement, evaluate), and it should be familiar to nurses.

Population health management also involves local, state, and federal government agencies and their staff. Policies and legislation related to health direct this work. Funding for these services is mostly provided through government budgets, although other sources may be used, such as grants and donations. When health services are provided, health insurance may cover some of these services. The most effective initiatives for population health engage as many relevant stakeholders as possible, use planning based on assessment, implement plans effectively and efficiently, and consider evaluation of outcomes throughout the process. Consumers should be involved, with their feedback used to improve services. Change in communities and populations is frequent, which means population health efforts must adjust and adapt when needed.

Typical healthcare providers (individuals and organizations) that are part of population health management are healthcare providers, such as physicians, nurses, pharmacists, social workers, and technicians; health systems and hospitals; post-acute care providers; public health agencies; and social and community services. Examples of specific interventions and programs that might be used to achieve positive population health outcomes include wellness screenings, health education programs, immunization clinics, 24/7 nurse helplines, smoking-cessation programs, support groups, disease management, **case management** (coordinate patient's care to ensure outcomes are met), home healthcare, long-term care services, medical homes, and clinics (e.g., public health department, retail clinics, nurse-managed clinics, federally qualified health centers, and accountable care organizations).

Population Health Measurement

Effective population health management requires routine measurement to identify gaps or needs and outcomes. This assessment should be planned and requires clear communication and sharing of information with all who need the information. Key measurement principles (Steifel & Nolan, 2012, p. 2) focus on the need for:

- A defined population
- Data over time
- Distinguishing between outcome and process measures
- Distinguishing between population and project measures
- Recognition of the value of benchmark or comparison data

Measurement should emphasize the Triple Aim (care, health, and cost) and STEEEP®, the six aims of improvement (safe, timely, effective, efficient, equitable, and patient-centered).

Measurement requires effective systems. Public health **surveillance** is used by communities to detect problems by using continuous, systematic collection of data for analysis and interpretation. This information is then used for planning, implementation, and evaluation of public health services (HHS, Health Resources & Services Administration [HRSA], 2019).

A patient **registry** is one tool that can be used to better ensure population health and in population health management and measurement. This type of registry is "an organized system that uses observational study methods to collect uniform data (clinical and other) to evaluate specified outcomes for a population defined by a particular disease, condition, or exposure, and that serves one or more predetermined scientific, clinical, or policy purposes"

(HHS, Agency for Healthcare Research and Quality [AHRQ], 2021). How might a registry be used? Later in this guide vulnerable populations' health needs and outcomes are discussed. Population health management is used with these populations, but it is important to have information about the vulnerable population in order to plan, provide care and services, and evaluate outcomes. A registry is one method that might be used to assist in this process.

Telehealth is now used more in acute care and has been developed to meet a variety of healthcare service needs. As more emphasis is placed on public and community health and services, such as population health management, new approaches will also be used in this area of care. Telehealth has expanded into population health. Nurses need to be involved in this development as they have expertise about patient care and communication and should also serve as telehealth providers. They need to consider how telehealth can assist more populations in a variety of situations and should also participate in evaluating new approaches to healthcare delivery, such as telehealth in public and community health.

Major Vulnerable Populations and Relationships to Public and Community Health, Social Determinants of Health, Health Equity, and Disparities

Vulnerable populations are groups of people who share characteristics and are at higher risk for health problems and poor outcomes, and the influence of SDOH should be considered in assessing and meeting their needs. There are many vulnerable populations, and they vary a great deal, although some people may be included in several vulnerable populations, such as teens experiencing SUD or older adults with disabilities. This section describes some of these populations, including populations with chronic health problems; populations with special medical needs (e.g., those who are immunosuppressed, people who have undergone organ transplantation, people with disabilities); children and teens; pregnant women; older adults; the LGBTQ+ (lesbian, gay, bisexual, transgender, and queer or questioning) population; racial and ethnic minority populations; socioeconomically disadvantaged populations; the homeless population; refugees, migrants, and immigrants; rural populations; persons who experience mental health problems and/or SUD; and vulnerable populations and communities who experience violence or abuse.

Vulnerable Populations and Social Determinants of Health, Health Equity, and Disparities

Diversity is a term describing differences in population characteristics, such as gender, religion, ethnicity, and age, among other types. Vulnerable populations are diverse, and this diversity is an important factor to consider within the public and community perspective. In addition, **health disparities** are found in these populations. These disparities are "preventable differences in the burden of disease, injury, violence, or in opportunities to achieve optimal health experienced by socially disadvantaged racial, ethnic, and other population groups, and communities. Health disparities exist in all age groups, including older adults" (HHS, CDC, 2017).

Certain factors, such as gender, age, or income, can influence an individual's health, risk for certain diseases, and risk for being seriously affected by public health emergencies (e.g., floods, major storms, fires, epidemics). This also applies to specific vulnerable populations. Effective population health management for vulnerable populations includes the following (HHS, CDC, 2022b):

- Identify populations or geographies likely to be at risk for acute and chronic illnesses or exposed to various potentially harmful chemicals in the environment.
- Gage a community's preparedness and potential impact due to a public health emergency.
- Better understand the factors that influence environmental exposures and human health across the United States.
- Assess the magnitude of county-level disparities over time.
- Monitor the effects of public health policies aimed at lessening the environmental burden on various populations.
- Make informed decisions about resources needed for public health response or public safety by:
  - Identifying community-specific threats and hazards, at-risk populations, and community vulnerabilities
  - Evaluating possible scenarios based on time, place, and conditions
  - Determining potential resource needs and public health actions which could mitigate or prevent illness, injury, and death

The CDC and HHS Office of Minority Health (OMH) developed the Minority Health Social Vulnerability Index (SVI) to identify racial and ethnic minority communities at greatest risk for disproportionate impact and adverse outcomes due to the COVID-19 pandemic. The information was then used to assess more effectively the use of existing resources, and in 2021 the SVI was revised. *Social vulnerability* "refers to the potential negative effects on communities caused by external stresses on human health. Such stresses include natural or human-caused disasters or disease outbreaks. Reducing social vulnerability can decrease both human suffering and economic loss" (HHS, CDC, OMH, 2021). The revised version includes additional variables for race, ethnicity, language, medical vulnerability, and healthcare infrastructure.

The American Public Health Association (APHA) recognizes that policies and practices may create an unequal distribution of money, power, and resources among communities based on factors such as race, class, gender, and location and may lead to inequities. It is important to assess and address SDOH and inequities (APHA, 2021a). This applies to vulnerable populations who often experience inequities such as structural or systemic racism and associated discrimination (Baily et al., 2021). The World Health Organization (WHO) defines SDOH as "conditions in which people are born, grow, live, work, and age" (WHO, 2021a). SDOH are factors that are not directly associated with health but can have a negative impact on health and outcomes. Determinant categories or contexts include (HHS, Office of Disease Prevention and Health Promotion [ODPHP], 2020):

- **Social and community context** (e.g., demographics, social networks and supports; social cohesion; racial, ethnic, religious, and gender discrimination; community safety; criminal justice climate; civil participation)
- **Economic stability** (e.g., employment, income, poverty)
- **Education access and quality** (e.g., quality of daycare, schools, and adult education; literacy and high school graduation rates; English proficiency)
- **Neighborhood and built environment** (e.g., housing, transportation, workplace safety, food availability, accessibility of parks and other recreational facilities, environmental conditions, sufficiency of social services)
- **Healthcare access and quality** (e.g., access to high-quality, culturally and linguistically appropriate, and health-literate care; access to health insurance; healthcare laws and policies; health promotion initiatives; availability of services; attitudes toward healthcare; and use of services)

Healthy People 2030 includes information on the SDOH. Review the link below and summarize key points you think are important for you to remember and apply. Additional information can be found in **Appendix B**.

    Website: https://health.gov/healthypeople/objectives-and-data/social-determinants-health

Major Common Problems Experienced by Vulnerable Populations and Their Impact on Public and Community Health

Each vulnerable population has some problems that are unique to the population, but there are also common challenges or those that many vulnerable populations are at risk of experiencing. Examples include:

- Physical health
- Psychological
- Socioeconomic
- Behavioral

This list provides a guide for surveillance and monitoring of problems in vulnerable populations. Public and community health staff need to consider these risk areas when planning and implementing services for vulnerable populations and outcomes should be monitored in the evaluation process.

Major Vulnerable Populations

The following provides brief descriptions of common vulnerable populations that are important in public and community health and the nursing services provided to these populations.

Population With Chronic Health Problems

Chronic diseases are those that last for one year or longer, require medical treatment, and may limit activities of daily living. They can occur in any age group, and there is diversity in the types of people who experience chronic diseases. Conditions such as these include heart disease, stroke, cancer, diabetes, chronic lung disease, Alzheimer's disease, and chronic kidney disease, all of which impact disability and mortality. Chronic diseases represent the health problem with the largest impact on healthcare costs—$3.8 trillion annually (HHS, CDC, 2021b). Six out of 10 adults in the United States have a chronic disease, and four in 10 have more than one chronic disease, which complicates their needs and treatment.

Public health must consider behaviors that increase risk for chronic diseases, such as smoking and exposure to secondhand smoke, alcohol use, poor nutrition, and limited physical activity. Effective public health departments use surveillance to track the prevalence of these behaviors and chronic diseases (i.e., population health measurement); the data are then used in population health management.

Interventions that communities use to address these problems focus on several areas. Examples of environmental interventions include ensuring smoke-free areas in public sites and workplaces, increasing prices of unhealthy food products, monitoring air and water quality, and providing better access to healthy foods (e.g., increasing accessibility to food stores). The health system needs to coordinate care across settings, from acute care to public and community health, as vulnerable populations have complex needs. Examples of interventions with this focus include providing health screenings and immunizations, health education, and case management and monitoring people with diabetes and hypertension, for example. Public and community health services use a variety of methods to reach more people, particularly vulnerable populations. Some examples are retail clinics to provide easy access within neighborhoods, nurse-managed clinics, screenings at fairs and in shopping malls, reminders about smoking, guidance for effective access to healthcare insurance coverage, and wraparound services so that when someone goes for medical care, social services and often health insurance and legal guidance are available. Consumer health education can be offered in a variety of settings, including schools and religious institutions and may use face-to-face experiences (individual and groups), written material, information on the Internet and other devices, advertising such as signage (e.g., signs on highways to reduce speed and wear seatbelts), and media such as print, radio, and television.

Review the information on prevention of chronic diseases at the link below. Within your student teams, select one of the identified areas and discuss a plan that a nursing team in a community might use to prevent a chronic disease.
Website: https://www.cdc.gov/chronicdisease/about/prevent/index.htm

Populations With Special Medical Needs: Immunosuppressed, Organ Transplantation, Disabilities

There are many complex health needs that lead to vulnerable populations. Three identified here are persons with immunosuppression, persons who have undergone organ transplantation, and persons with disabilities.

Immunosuppression

"People who are immunosuppressed have a reduced ability to fight infections and other diseases" (National Institutes of Health [NIH], National Cancer Institute [NCI], 2022). There are many causes for this complex problem, including HIV and AIDS, cancer, diabetes, malnutrition, and certain genetic disorders as well as drugs or treatments, such as chemotherapy, radiation therapy, and stem cell or organ transplants. This condition may also be referred to as *being immunocompromised*. People with immunosuppression have a weakened immune system and, as such, are at greater risk of infections and complications.

This population is vulnerable, with many health risks, many long-term that need to be considered in the overall health needs of and services for those affected. In addition, because immunosuppression may be a long-term and complex problem, it affects general health, physical and psychological, and has social needs implications. For example, this health problem may impact employment, and the SDOH must also be considered. During the COVID-19 pandemic, immunosuppression was mentioned in relation to protecting those at high risk for COVID-19 who were less able to fight the infection. It was also discussed in terms of public health interventions such as social distancing and masking in public areas, where it is not easy to identify those who might be at more risk. People with immunosuppression also comprise a population for whom vaccines are critical, which requires careful assessment. The public has a responsibility to consider those at high risk—people who are vulnerable to getting an infection and may have more dangerous outcomes.

Organ Transplantation

People who need and/or receive organ transplants represent a vulnerable population. The most transplanted organs are the kidney, liver, heart, lungs, pancreas, and intestines, and the most transplanted tissues are bones, tendons, ligaments, heart valves, blood vessels, and corneas (HHS, CDC, 2019a). Waiting for transplantation can be a long and stressful process with a complex written consent process as well as screening and testing. Around 75,000 people are on transplant wait lists every day. Donors are required, and organ transplantation is an emotional process for the donors and their families. If the donors are living, they then are at risk for changes in their health. There are strict protocols that must be followed by healthcare systems and providers. Organ transplant patients are at risk for infections or organ rejection, making them very vulnerable. "The CDC has responsibility for surveillance, detection, and warning of potential public health risks within the organ and tissue supply. These public health efforts support initiatives that make transplants safe by reducing the potential for transmission of communicable diseases" (HHS, CDC, 2019b). As is the case with other vulnerable populations, we need to be alert for disparities and ensure health equity throughout the transplant process. The need for and receiving an organ transplant have a major impact on all aspects of a person's life. The healthcare system needs to consider the complexity of this experience, including the psychological, physical, social, and economic implications (NAM, 2022b).

Disabilities

One in four adults in the United States has some type of disability, and children also have disabilities (HHS, CDC, 2020a). The common types of problems that persons with disabilities experience are related to (HHS, CDC, 2020b):

- **Mobility:** Serious difficulty climbing stairs or walking
- **Cognition:** Serious difficulty concentrating, remembering, or making decisions
- **Independent living:** Difficulty doing errands alone
- **Hearing:** Deafness or serious difficulty hearing.
- **Vision:** Blindness or serious difficulty seeing
- **Self-care:** Difficulty dressing or bathing

When communities assess this vulnerable population, they should note that this is a diverse population—for example, two in five adults who are age 65 or older; one in four women; and two in five non-Hispanic, American Indians/Alaska Natives. This population often has health problems associated with obesity, smoking, heart disease, and diabetes, which increase their health problems, risks, and needs. Access to care may be a problem. This indicates that communities need ongoing assessment of this vulnerable population as well as planning to meet their ongoing health and social needs. See **Figure 1**.

Children and Teens

It is critical to promote health and prevent disease in all children and teenagers and ensure equity. The CDC notes that "a child's health is the public's health" (HHS, CDC, 2021a), and children and teens are the most prevalent vulnerable population. Children and teens of all ages are vulnerable to health problems, and in some cases, if they develop health problems, they will carry these issues into adulthood. Their risks are increased by the status of their family's health and socioeconomic issues. The HHS and the HRSA conduct the National Survey of Children's Health, and the 2019–2020 data indicated the following (HHS, HRSA, 2021a):

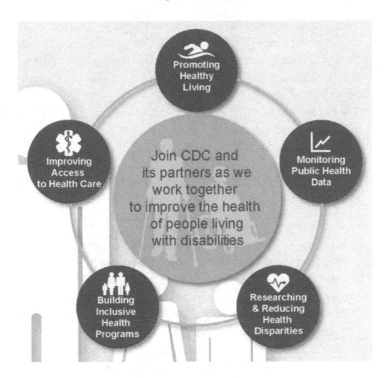

Figure 1. Making a Difference: Public Health for All of Us. Source: https://www.cdc.gov/ncbddd/disabilityandhealth/infographic-disability-impacts-all.html.

1. Usual source of preventive care

- Nearly 66 million, or 90.6%, of U.S. children ages 0–17 years had a place they usually went for routine preventive care, such as a well-child visit.
- The proportion of children with a usual source of preventive care was highest among non-Hispanic White (94.6%) and multiracial (94.7%) children and lowest among non-Hispanic Asian (82.5%) and Pacific Islander/Native Hawaiian (82.0%) children.
- The proportion of children with a usual source of preventive care increased as household income increased, from 82.0% at less than 100% of the federal poverty level (FPL) to 96.2% at 400% of the FPL or greater.

2. General health status

- Nearly 66 million, or 90.4%, of U.S. children ages 0–17 years were in excellent or very good health, as reported by a caregiver.

- Non-Hispanic White (93.4%) and non-Hispanic, multiracial (91.2%) children were most likely to be in excellent or very good health.
- Non-Hispanic American Indian/Alaska Native (84.1%) and non-Hispanic Black (85.9%) children were least likely to be in excellent or very good health.
- The percentage of children in excellent or very good health increased with household income, from 82.8% among those living in poverty (less than 100% of the FPL) to 95.4% among those living in households with incomes of 400% of the FPL or higher.
- About 1 million (1.5%) of children were reported to be in poor or fair health.

The data indicate that there are health problems across ages and that diversity is a factor that must be considered. An area of child and teen health that often goes unrecognized is injury. Injury is the leading cause of death in children in the United States and is associated with millions of children requiring treatment in the emergency department. It is important for communities to assess safety risk (such as at playgrounds, at school bus stops, and when walking to school, and in terms of fire risk in homes and schools). Safety education should be provided to children, school staff, and families. School nurses should be alert to safety issues, including the use of substances by children and their families, violence, abuse, and emotional stress.

Health problems as well as family and SDOH issues affect school attendance. We have seen during the COVID-19 pandemic the impact of closing schools or reducing attendance by either the school or due to parents' decisions and the use of virtual classrooms. It is not yet clear what the long-term impact will be, but during this time many children and teens did not have access to school health services, support services and assessment, regular exercise, and nutrition during the day. In addition, they lost opportunity for social development and experienced isolation from peers, a critical factor in childhood that then influences adulthood. For children and teens in minority populations, the negative impact has been greater. For example, for children who may not yet speak English, they lost time in developing this important skill, which is needed in childhood and adulthood. Often their families do not speak English well, and thus school is where their language skills are developed.

Prior to COVID-19, childhood mortality was decreasing globally, but the virus has led to more deaths in this vulnerable population who also were not able to receive vaccines early when vaccines were first available in the pandemic. For some ages and in some countries, children had no opportunity to receive vaccines, or parents refused vaccines for their children. Along with concerns about the pandemic and the unknown of future epidemics, there are growing health concerns for children and teens. "Children (aged 0 to 18 years) today face a host of new threats linked to climate change, pollution, harmful commercial marketing, unhealthy lifestyles and diets, injury and violence, conflict, migration, and inequality. Their very future is uncertain, and urgent action is needed to address these threats" (WHO, 2020). In addition, as noted in the section on refugees, there is concern for children within the refugee population. In 2022, war in Europe resulted in major crises for many people, and among them were many children who fled with their mothers and grandmothers to safety—leaving behind fathers and other male relatives. The most vulnerable confronted the greatest number of challenges. How will this affect their physical health, development, mental health, and long-term education? These children experienced extreme stress, fear and loss, limited nutrition and water, long hours in the cold, and separation from loved ones and their homes and schools. Long-term public health services will need to deal with these problems. The United States did not experience the war directly, but U.S. parents may hear from their children who have seen photos, heard stories, and viewed Internet information. Children and teens now encounter a greater amount of information. Children seeing children suffer has an impact on all children. As has been said in this content, *vulnerable* means at risk, and this means adults must be alert. In the United States, school nurses, who have carried a heavy burden in working with children of all ages and their caregivers and COVID-19 concerns, may encounter children who fear leaving home as well as all the losses that could happen to them and their families. Prevention and openness in talking about these fears is critical, but first, parents, teachers, school administrators, and school health staff must be on alert and ready to assess.

Common health problems for children and teens of which caregivers and public and community health providers should be aware are obesity (which increases the risk of other health problems, such as heart, diabetes, and respiratory issues, and places limits on exercise; it also may increase the risks of depression and bullying), substance use (e.g., drugs, alcohol), bullying, stress and anxiety, Internet safety, smoking, teen pregnancy, child abuse and neglect, and depression (Healthgrades, 2020). Another health concern that is connected to environmental health is allergies and associated asthma. Children with developmental disabilities are at particular risk and need regular assessment, treatment, and preventive care. Quality of housing (i.e., SDOH) is a critical factor in increasing the risk of allergies and asthma in children. See the other vulnerable population sections on chronic health, mental health, substance use, violence, and disabilities, as these also apply to children and teens.

Children and teens require regular assessment and preventive care, including immunizations. The responsibility for ensuring these occur lies with the family and caregivers; however, public and community health providers and individual providers and services and organizations are also accountable for providing accessible and effective services, including assessment, treatment, coordination, and follow-up. Communities must place this vulnerable population at the top of the list for risk and needs and recognize the impact of SDOH on health outcomes. Children and teens cannot speak for themselves, so others must routinely do so.

One approach that is now being discussed is the need for greater health literacy and health education in schools (Auld et al., 2020). Integrating health promotion and disease prevention into K–12 education supports the CDC health education standards (HHS, CDC, 2020c):

1. Students will comprehend concepts related to health promotion and disease prevention to enhance health.
2. Students will analyze the influence of family, peers, culture, media, technology, and other factors on health behaviors.
3. Students will demonstrate the ability to access valid information, products, and services to enhance health.
4. Students will demonstrate the ability to use interpersonal communication skills to enhance health and avoid or reduce health risks.
5. Students will demonstrate the ability to use decision-making skills to enhance health.
6. Students will demonstrate the ability to use goal-setting skills to enhance health.
7. Students will demonstrate the ability to practice health-enhancing behaviors and avoid or reduce health risks.
8. Students will demonstrate the ability to advocate for personal, family, and community health.

All initiatives that provide health education need to consider individual values, attitudes, and beliefs while ensuring health equity. Monitoring outcomes for this type of strategy can be done through Healthy People 2030, the HHS initiative that identifies objectives and assesses outcomes.

This section has discussed children and teens, but we should also recognize that the transition for late teens to adulthood is a critical time and that their experiences and health status transfer into early adulthood. It is acknowledged that education and employment affect health and overall well-being. Connected teens are engaged first in their education and then later in employment. When teens who do not live in poverty are compared to those who do, the former population has twice the rate of engagement or connectedness. Teens who live in poverty experience poorer health, lower-quality education, less access to transportation, and more violence and trauma in addition to having a higher rate of disabilities and experiencing family problems such as divorce and living with a single parent. Their risk is influenced by individual factors, family, community (e.g., violence and poverty in neighborhoods), and societal factors such as discrimination (APHA, 2021b). Indicators of major problems in this vulnerable population are lower high school and college graduate rates, an increased rate of living in institutional group settings (e.g., psychiatric and correctional facilities), and a higher rate of developing preventable health problems, such as diabetes and hypertension. This population also is more likely to use government financial support, such as Medicaid and Temporary Assistance for Needy Families. In summary, these are teens who have multiple risk factors that typically lead to poor outcomes in health as well as greater social needs, with concerns related to SDOH in their lives, and then they enter early adulthood with complex physical, psychological, and social difficulties.

Pregnant Women

Pregnant women are considered a vulnerable population because of the risks for the fetus and the newborn. As noted earlier, research requires identification of vulnerable populations who may have limited decision-making in terms of research consent. Some have commented that pregnant women should not be considered a vulnerable population, at least from the research perspective. Pregnancy does not limit women in giving consent for research (Krubiner & Faden, 2017). From a health perspective, however, pregnant women and their unborn children as well as during postpartum experiences are at risk for health problems and challenges to their social well-being. This population is unique in that the fetus and then the newborn is dependent on the mother or another caregiver (Barlow, 2015). The fetus is affected not only by physical factors such as health of the mother, nutrition, and more, but also by psychosocial factors and SDOH. For example, when pregnant women and new mothers experience anxiety or depression, this affects the newborn. Use of substances, including smoking and consuming alcohol, is also a serious concern, as substance use affects the mother, fetus, and newborn.

Healthy People 2030 includes the following goal: "Prevent pregnancy complications and maternal deaths and improve women's health before, during, and after pregnancy" (HHS, ODPHP, 2022a). It may come as a surprise, but there is a higher risk for death during childbirth in the United States than in other developed countries (GBD [Global Burden of Disease]

2015 Maternal Mortality Collaborators, 2016). Woman may have health problems before pregnancy, may experience issues only during pregnancy, or may have health challenges that either continue after or begin at delivery. Healthy habits are important for women during pregnancy and postpartum. Women also need regular assessments to ensure the health of the mother and child; however, many factors related to SDOH may limit access to this care, such as a lack of finances for services, lack of transportation to healthcare services, an unhealthy diet, and lack of safety at home.

Review the Healthy People 2030 link on pregnancy and childbirth to review the objectives related to this health need. How are the goals categorized? Click on several objectives and review the information. How does the information relate to public and community health nursing for this vulnerable population?
Website: https://health.gov/healthypeople/objectives-and-data/browse-objectives/pregnancy-and-childbirth

Older Adults

Healthy People 2030 includes the goal of improving health and well-being for older adults (HHS, ODPHP, 2021a). By 2060, almost a quarter of the U.S. population will be age 65 or older, which means there is a great need to respond to this vulnerable population now and prepare plans for response in the future. This population has a high rate of chronic health problems such as diabetes, osteoporosis, and Alzheimer's disease, all of which require regular monitoring and treatment and affect all aspects of a person's life. Falls are also a frequent concern, with one in three experiencing falls each year, some of which lead to long-term mobility problems as well as other health and social issues, such as isolation and fear of leaving the home. As has been noted earlier, during the COVID-19 pandemic, the older adult population was at higher risk of getting the virus, requiring hospitalization, and dying. This population has a higher risk of infection in general, particularly for those who are hospitalized. Other common healthcare concerns including having sensory and communication disorders, respiratory disease, osteoporosis or arthritis, or mental health problems (e.g., anxiety and depression). Older adults also experience SUD, which may be a long-term problem or develop later in life. Obesity is also an issue that affects other health conditions and quality of life (Callahan et al., 2022). As is relevant with all vulnerable populations, cultural determinants of health and SDOH have an impact on the health status of older adults.

Preventive care is important. Communities need to provide immunizations, both routine and special (e.g., for COVID-19). Services provided must be easily accessible during hours that are reasonable for older adults. All services must consider potential mobility issues, provide waiting areas with seating, have staff to assess patients' status and insurance coverage for care, and offer easy access to pharmacies to get medications. (For example, some pharmacies now offer home delivery, and orders can be made via the Internet.) Older adults may use more home healthcare services and have a greater interest in aging at home rather than moving to a long-term care facility. Food insecurity or limited access to nutritional and safe foods is a problem for many older adults due to costs and often limitations to access to food sources for shopping (Shaunna et al., 2020). This alone is a major health concern as nutrition is necessary for healthy living; however, some older adults with limited funds must choose between paying for food or medications and therefore, understandably, may choose food and forego taking the medications they need. Nonadherence to medication use is a community problem as these adults live in all types of communities. Red flags for this problem include low income, health insurance gaps, and higher out-of-pocket prescription costs (Shaunna et al., 2020). This issue requires communities and public health providers to be alert to this risk, assess carefully, educate older adults about the need for nutrition and prescribed medications taken as prescribed in the amount ordered, and, when possible, alert family members and caregivers. Funds for both food and prescriptions need to be assessed as well as other sources to assist and meet needs.

With the development of telehealth, older adults may be major users of this service in their homes; however, having the access and ability to use the technology is important to take into consideration when planning these services. In addition, the older adult population typically prefers personal contact, a factor that must be considered for all services, including telehealth.

Locations that provide long-term care services are also important community healthcare sites—they are deemed as such because they are places where some older adults live in addition to receiving care. Long-term care should be considered a part of public and community health.

With the increasing size of the older adult population, more attention is being given to their needs in healthcare systems. The term *age-friendly health systems* is now in usage. Several organizations, including the John A. Hartford Foundation, Institute for Healthcare Improvement (IHI), AHA, and Catholic Hospital Association, have developed an age-friendly systems movement that has recognized more than 2,700 care organizations for meeting effective criteria for this population (IHI, 2022). These standards focus on the 4 M's: asking what *matters* to older adults, *medication*, *mentation*, and *mobility*. This focus tends to be oriented on hospitals and long-term care facilities, but what about public health? Within this area, it has not been ignored; for example, "[the] county health departments in Florida participating in the pilot are leveraging the *Framework* to expand public health practice, programs, and policies that address health services and health behaviors, social, and economic factors and environmental conditions that allow older adults to age in place and live healthier and more productive lives" (De Biasi et al., 2020; Wolfe et al., 2021). Hopefully, more health departments will participate in implementing changes.

Older adults who do not live in a structured setting such as a long-term care facility may require personal care in their home. This can be a burden to families, and some older adults do not have families or families who live nearby. Home healthcare services can be an asset for some patients, but providing these requires funds to cover the costs, and these services are limited. However, many older adults live in their own home and experience self-care, receive periodic care from providers in their home, or seek care outside their home when required (e.g., at a clinic or from a private doctor). People within this population take many medications for various conditions. This leads to concern about medication safety in the home and the need to ensure that older adults have access to required medications and can cover costs; understand what they need to take, the amount, and their medication schedule; can open medication easily; monitor medication when they take it to reduce the risk of accidental overdose or missing a dose; and know how to access a healthcare provider if they need to ask questions. If the older adult agrees—as consent is required unless the person no longer has legal control over decisions —families and caregivers also may be involved. Communities need to provide access to education on medication safety in the home. When care providers (registered nurses and home healthcare assistants or aides) make visits, they must check on their patients' medications and reinforce medication safety.

To gain a better understanding of the needs of this population, the following data were compiled and describe the typical long-term services required for adults ages 65 and older (HHS, CDC, National Center for Health Statistics [NCHS], 2022):

- Percentage of adult day services center participants: 62.5% (2016)
- Percentage of home health agency patients: 81.9% (2015)
- Percentage of hospice patients: 94.6% (2015)
- Percentage of nursing home residents: 83.5% (2016)
- Percentage of residential care community residents: 93.4% (2016)

Communities may offer various services for older adults. Some of these include adult daycare centers, exercise groups in community centers or other locations such as parks and even walking groups in malls, support groups, and social services. Ideally, the latter should be offered as wraparound services accessible in clinics and include social, legal, and health coverage information (e.g., information related to Medicare).

Another service important for the older adult population focuses on the transitional care model. When older adults are hospitalized and then discharged, the handoff period is critical for effective long-term progress. The transitional care model, which is supported by the Centers for Medicare & Medicaid (CMS) as a valuable approach to care, includes post-hospital transitioning to the home, home care services, a nursing home, or an assisted living facility. The goal is to prevent complications and rehospitalization. This all requires community collaboration and coordination from all relevant stakeholders.

Family caregivers struggle greatly when helping older family members. Paid leave is a strategy for helping them take time off from work to give support and care. As of early 2022, seven states and Washington, DC, offered paid leave, a provision based on state, not federal, legislation. Two other states plan to initiate this policy in 2023–2024. Fewer than a quarter of U.S. workers have access to paid leave (AARP, 2022). AARP recommends a national policy on this issue as it is a growing problem for many families.

Age bias, or stereotyping and discrimination due to age, is an important concern. In some situations, healthcare providers and social service staff demean older adults by using language that makes the patients feel weak and childlike, for example. Attitudes toward aging affect this type of response. When possible, older adults must be included in decision-making. Neglecting to do so can lower their self-esteem and may cause them to become anxious or depressed and feel isolated. One risk due to this type of negative interaction is that the individuals may neglect sharing important information related to their needs, which could limit effective assessment and intervention. Family members may also demonstrate age bias, which can have the same impact on older adult family members and also negatively affect family relationships, trust, and communication. Ageism is associated with negative physical and psychological health. "Ageism refers to the stereotypes (how we think), prejudice (how we feel) and discrimination (how we act) towards others or oneself based on age. Who does ageism affect? Ageism affects everyone. Children as young as 4 years old become aware of their culture's age stereotypes" (WHO, 2021b). To address this global problem, WHO recommends three interventions. The first is to develop and implement policies and laws to reduce discrimination and inequality related to age, which will help protect human rights. Second, education is needed to increase knowledge about aging and reduce prejudice. The third intervention is to offer opportunities for intergenerational interaction. Some communities encourage this through having older adults and children and teens interact while at school or in long-term care settings or adult daycare centers.

LGBTQ+ Population

The LGBTQ+ (defined earlier in the text) population is one that is vulnerable and at risk for mental, emotional, behavioral, and physical problems (NAM, 2022a). Individuals within this population are at risk due to SDOH and experience inequalities at school, at work, and within communities, including the healthcare system, acute care, and public and community health; they also often experience problems with their family and peer relationships. Just as is true with other vulnerable populations, the LGBTQ+ population is racially, ethnically, and socioeconomically diverse.

LGBTQ+ children and teens encounter many issues with discrimination in schools, which adds to their stress. School is a place within communities where children of all ages should feel safe, and, when this is not the case, it impacts all other aspects of the involved individuals' lives. School staff need to be knowledgeable about this vulnerable population, assess needs, and respond with effective, supportive interventions. Parents must also be included.

Another area of concern for LGBTQ+ children is where they live. Compared to other children and teens, they are disproportionately represented in multiple state-based systems, such as the foster care system and juvenile justice system. This increases their risk for abuse—physical, psychological, and sexual (NAM, 2022a).

Communities must be aware of the needs of this vulnerable population and assess, prevent immediate and long-term problems, and intervene when needed to support them. This requires collaboration and coordination with local policies, schools, community group and social activities, employers, social services, and healthcare. Providing support and education to families is also a critical element for the LGBTQ+ population. Reducing discrimination should be a particular focus. Assessment and planning should consider the following possible problems:

- Depression and anxiety
- Bullying in school
- Violence (from others, to others, within the family, and the risk of suicide)
- Sexual abuse and/or assault
- Substance use
- Academic performance
- Sexually transmitted diseases and other infections
- Typical health problems found per age group
- Legal discrimination (e.g., in housing and employment)

Many states and cities now offer LGBTQ+ clinics to provide services that meet the physical, psychological, and social needs of this population. These clinics should be locations with acceptance and where the patients feel safe to obtain help and support (HHS, CDC, 2021c).

It is important to monitor the status of this vulnerable population in order to respond effectively to their needs. Healthy People 2030 includes the goal of improving "the health, safety, and well-being of lesbian, gay, bisexual, and transgender people" (HHS, ODPHP, 2021b). Specific objectives related to this goal are being actively monitored.

Review the information on the Healthy People 2030 objectives regarding the LGBTQ+ population. What are the objectives and their status?
Website: https://health.gov/healthypeople/objectives-and-data/browse-objectives/lgbt

Racial and Ethnic Minority Populations

"Racism is a system consisting of structures, policies, practices, and norms—that assigns value and determines opportunity based on the way people look or the color of their skin. This results in conditions that unfairly advantage some and disadvantage others throughout society" (HHS, CDC, Office of Minority Health & Health Equity, 2021). Racism is not always conscious or intentional and can be integrated within systems, policies, and laws (Robert Wood Johnson Foundation [RWJF], 2022). The phenomenon is a serious threat to U.S. public health, and, although it is not new, it has increased and affects where and how people live and work. Racism also impacts poor health outcomes. The CDC notes that "to build a healthier America for all, we must confront the systems and policies that have resulted in the generational injustice that has given rise to racial and ethnic health inequities" (HHS, CDC, 2021d). Racism is a barrier to health equity and to reducing health disparities. It impacts inequities in the following ways: poverty level; housing and access to safe housing; quality education and safety for children and staff, social activities, employment, and access to food and other needs; healthcare services; increased risk for crime—as victim or for criminal behavior; environment (e.g., air quality, clean water, hazardous waste, lead exposure, exposure to rodents, risk of fires); negative relationships; and risk with the police and justice system. These experiences may lead to chronic stress and health problems. Health equity is critical—all people have the same right and opportunity to be as healthy as possible. **Figure 2** describes the HHS's and CDC's view regarding how to achieve health equity.

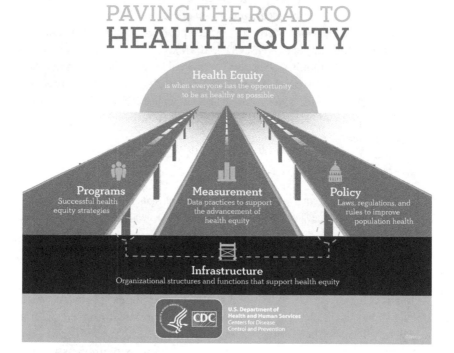

Figure 2.   Paving the Road to Health Equity. Source: https://www.cdc.gov/minorityhealth/publications/health_equity/Health_Equity_Infographic.pdf.

Socioeconomically Disadvantaged Population

The HHS through the CDC emphasizes the need to recognize the connection between community health and economic prosperity. In 2022, the U.S. Surgeon General issued a report titled *Community Health and Economic Prosperity: Engaging Businesses as Stewards and Stakeholders* (HHS, CDC, 2022c). This was the first time this type of report had been developed. The report is significant as it "raises awareness of the U.S. health disadvantage and demonstrates to business leaders the opportunity investing in community health can bring to the business bottom line and the health of the economy" (HHS, CDC, 2022c). The report focused on three concerns (HHS, CDC, 2022c):

- The U.S. health disadvantage and the burden it places on businesses and the economy (in addition to people and families)
- How communities can become (or improve as) places that nurture health, wealth, and well-being and offer children and families opportunities to thrive
- The meaning and role of businesses in the United States and how businesses can create value for themselves and their communities by

helping address the conditions that drive poor health and creating conditions that help people thrive

Population health and the health of vulnerable populations is directly connected to SDOH, as is economic stability. The report highlights "the goal of helping people to earn steady incomes that allow them to meet their health needs" (HHS, ODPHP, 2021c). With one in 10 people living in poverty in the United States, there is a need to recognize that poverty exists and has a negative impact on health and healthy living (Semega et al., 2019). This is a major risk factor, not only for physical health but also for well-being and mental health. Economic status also affects behavior related to substance use, crime and violence, family stability, school performance, and employment. Health insurance is a critical factor in effective access to care when needed. In the United States, most health insurance is connected to employment, so a lack thereof or employment that does not offer health insurance is a barrier. The other choices for health insurance are private plans, which are costly, and government coverage such as Medicare and Medicaid. The Affordable Care Act of 2010 increased these options; for example, by January 2022, enrollment via this program was estimated to be 14.5 million, and this number is increasing annually. Health insurance coverage has a direct impact on healthcare services and health status, as illustrated by the following data (Keisler-Starkey & Bunch, 2021):

- In 2020, 8.6% of people, or 28 million, did not have health insurance at any point during the year.
- The percentage of people with health insurance coverage for all or part of 2020 was 91.4%.
- In 2020, private health insurance coverage continued to be more prevalent than public coverage at 66.5% and 34.8%, respectively. Of the subtypes of health insurance coverage, employment-based insurance was the most common, covering 54.4% of the population for some or all of the entire calendar year, followed by Medicare (18.4%), Medicaid (17.8%), direct-purchase coverage (10.5%), TRICARE (2.8%), and Department of Veterans Affairs (VA) or Civilian Health and Medical Program of the VA coverage (0.9%).

COVID-19 has had a major impact on the socioeconomic status of many people across the United States due to loss of income from job loss or reduced work time. Concern about future employment and opportunities weigh heavily on many, affecting housing and family stability and increasing stress-related responses, such as substance use, crime, violence, and suicide. Homelessness and lack of stable housing have also increased. These factors raise the number of health risks for individuals, families, populations, and communities.

Homeless Populations

Housing is associated with health. People without secure, regular housing have a higher rate of health problems and, on average, die 12 years sooner on average than the general U.S. population. The reverse is also a concern in that poor health can lead to homelessness (e.g., due to loss of employment and health insurance leading to financial problems). We may see more of this as a result of the COVID-19 pandemic. Not having a home can be described as a dangerous health condition, as people with health problems get worse and people may develop new health conditions (National Health Care for the Homeless Council, 2019). Common health problems seen in this vulnerable population include diabetes, hypertension, heart attack, HIV and AIDS, hepatitis C, depression, and SUD. Safe, secure housing can help reduce the risk for these problems. Treatment for and prevention of health issues are critical, but without stable housing, treatment will not be successful in the long term. The needs of this population include all common health problems; however, homeless individuals are at particular risk for communicable diseases due to their living conditions and lack of healthy living habits as well as for stress and mental health concerns along with substance use (alcohol and drugs) and experiences with other at-risk behaviors, such as unsafe sexual behavior, abuse, and violence. It is important to recognize that this population includes all age groups, individuals, and families, and thus interventions to assist them must include a broad range of issues and approaches. "On a single night in January last year there were an estimated 553,000 individuals experiencing homelessness in the United States. Nearly 200,000 of these individuals were unsheltered, sleeping on sidewalks, in parks, in cars, or in other outdoor locations" (U.S. Department of Housing and Urban Development, Office of Policy Development and Research, 2020).

Lack of appropriate housing is a problem that requires more information to develop better responses and interventions. An example of research and assessment is the California Policy Lab analysis of responses from more than 64,000 adults in the United States experiencing both sheltered and unsheltered homelessness (Rountree et al., 2019). The term *sheltered homeless* refers to people with no permanent housing who use some type of community housing, such as a shelter, often during nighttime for sleep or during inclement weather. The data support the view that unsheltered adults report more problems from chronic health conditions, mental health issues, and experience with trauma and substance abuse problems as compared to homeless people in shelters, and their problems (e.g., health and social) worsen the longer they remain in an unsheltered situation. Women are particularly affected by this experience. This type of analysis should help communities as they make plans to address homeless populations and consider the impact of using various types of sheltered housing options. Communities need to understand that collecting data about this population is not easy and is typically incomplete. More research and assessment are needed, as the need for permanent housing is an SDOH that we need to understand further. "Future research should focus on documenting effective strategies for moving people from the street and shelters into permanent housing. People with the longest experiences of homelessness, most significant health conditions, and greatest vulnerabilities are not accessing or being served by emergency shelters" (Rountree et al., 2019, p. 7).

Other research indicates that, when homelessness is considered, many basic human needs in addition to health must be considered first, such as food and safe shelter. "Bureaucracy and rigid opening hours, as well as discrimination and stigma, hinder these persons' access to health- and social care" (Omerov et al., 2019). The healthcare structure may act as a barrier to access and trust with this population. Many have had negative and often discriminatory experiences with systems, a feeling of mistrust that then leads to avoidance of seeking help and following treatment advice for emergency health needs and chronic conditions (Liu & Hwang, 2021). People experiencing homelessness are often marginalized, having experienced healthcare interactions that left them feeling disrespected and unable to access care when needed. One example of a community-based participatory approach can be seen with the Healthcare for the Homeless Suitcase Clinic (Kiser & Hulton, 2018). The health service program provides unconventional portable, mobile clinic services referred to as *suitcase clinics* that use volunteer providers and have a nurse case manager. The program was initiated in five shelter settings in a rural mid-Atlantic community and represents a collaboration between practice organizations, local government, and academic partners.

There is a lot of information on vulnerable populations, but the homeless population is one about which nurses and nursing students often do not know much. Explore the link to learn about the National Healthcare for the Homeless Council and its activities. How do these activities relate to public and community health nursing?

Website: https://nhchc.org/clinical-practice/diseases-and-conditions/influenza/

Refugees, Migrants, and Immigrants

Refugees are people who leave their country due to disaster, violence/conflict/war, and other major crises, and often this is a sudden decision and one that results in a migration of people who often do not return home due to the risks. We have experienced this during the past few years, with refugees traveling from the Middle East to Europe. In 2019, there were 20.7 million refugees (men, women, children) globally and 5.7 million housed in camps in the Middle East. Refugees often travel long distances in extremely dangerous, often life-threatening, travel. More recently, the United States received refugees from Afghanistan. Refugees are highly vulnerable, arriving with health problems, emotional stress, little if any financial support, language difficulties, cultural and religious differences, and the need for education. They often come from cultures vastly different from that of the United States and are unprepared due to the crises that have motivated them to leave their home country. They do not necessarily apply for citizenship in the countries in which they seek refuge and may want to return home when their home country situation improves. In 2022, Russia attacked Ukraine, which led to a huge migration of refugees. An estimated 11 million, more than half of whom were children, left Ukraine in fear and under a difficult situation. This refugee group is different from those who traveled to Europe from the Middle East in the past few years, many of whom stayed. The Ukrainian refugee group is mostly composed of women, children, and elderly, with men remaining at home to fight. In addition, sick children traveling from hospitals and orphans leaving orphanages required complex support. There were also an estimated 7.1 million people displaced within their country, now homeless due to the war. Countries that help refugees carry heavy and usually sudden burdens to provide all basic needs to people who are highly stressed and have little or no money or even personal belongings. Their lives are suddenly upended with no work, school, friends, or typical social life. Language is also a critical issue. What they want is to feel safe.

The HHS and the U.S. Department of Homeland Security are involved in assisting refugees. The recent refugee group from Afghanistan is now settling into many U.S. communities. HHS has a website entitled Ethnic Community Self-Help. Review the site. What can you learn about this population and the services? Consider the impact of new people from different countries moving to a community and how it might affect public and community health services and your role as a nurse.
   Website: https://www.acf.hhs.gov/orr/programs/refugees/ethnic-community-self-help

Immigrants are somewhat different from refugees, although they may experience similar adjustment problems, often having been forced to make the choice to leave their home country permanently. Usually strong motivators exist, such as financial needs and the necessity for work or joining other family members, and immigrants may also have political concerns for their safety. These people apply for entrance (or should do so) to the new country.

Eventually they may become citizens. They have many needs that take time to resolve, such as housing, employment, adjustment to a new place and culture, language barriers, need for education, transportation, and healthcare. Religious practices may also be a concern for some, and thus they seek out areas to live where they can have this type of support.

Refugees and immigrants require healthcare coverage. Medicaid and other federal healthcare insurance programs assist with these costs to ensure services are available (HHS, CMS, 2021a). The Federal Emergency Management Agency (FEMA) is also involved in assisting individuals within this vulnerable population and their resettlement.

A migrant is someone who moves away, either temporarily or permanently, from their home country, crossing international borders. In the United States, agricultural and rural areas often have migrant workers, but they can also be found in urban areas. Health screening, assessment, and initiatives to reduce infectious diseases are part of the initial health services for this vulnerable population. For example, all immigrants are required to have a medical exam to receive an immigrant visa (HHS, CDC, 2021e). The Domestic Refugee Health Program collaborates with the Division of Global Migration and Quarantine, CDC, and its domestic partners, to "improve the healthcare of refugees after their arrival in the United States, initiate surveillance activities to monitor medical conditions identified post-arrival, work together to ensure adequate follow-up of refugees with medical conditions identified overseas, and strengthen the resources available for post-arrival health assessments and follow-up activities" (HHS, CDC, 2021e). Included in this process, the CDC works to promote and improve the health of immigrants, refugees, and migrants, including prevention of infectious diseases through screening and immunizations—for example, for tuberculosis, which is of concern not only for the people entering the United States but also for the local population. Mandatory health screenings for all immigrants and refugees entering the United States are used to identify health concerns and initiate care.

Rural Populations

Almost 60 million people in the United States live in rural areas, where they are limited in getting timely, quality, affordable care, as noted by the 2019 *National Healthcare Quality and Disparities Report* (NHQDR) (HHS, AHRQ, 2021). Rural communities tend to have older adults and thus more chronic illnesses that require regular healthcare, although often this care is unavailable (National Academy of Medicine, 2021a). Because taxes are an important source of community health services and often tax levels are low in rural areas, this may limit services and maintenance of services as well as funding for healthcare staff and social services. In general, it is difficult to attract healthcare providers to rural areas as many do not want to live away from urban centers for personal reasons but also due to the quality and level of healthcare facilities and their equipment and salary levels. Structural urbanism is prevalent, meaning there is greater interest and funding in providing urban healthcare (NAM, 2021a). When Medicare and Medicaid, the two major government healthcare coverage sources, are considered, they tend to focus on individual healthcare rather than population health, which has a negative impact on rural health. However, in late 2021, due to the impact of COVID-19, there was increased concern about rural health as rural communities needed extra funds to cope with the increased use of their hospitals and the influx in the number of critical patients. Rural hospitals and clinics received additional federal funding through the HHS and as part of the American Rescue Plan legislation, which provided $7.5 billion to more than 40,000 healthcare providers across the United States (HHS, 2021a). It is important to recognize that rural health has dealt with problems for a long time, but addressing them was not a top priority. A positive aspect of a crisis such as COVID-19 is that this type of experience sometimes increases awareness of long-term issues that should have been resolved earlier.

There is a difference in rural and urban mortality rates, with urban areas having lower rates. Factors that affect this include access to health services, SDOH, and population behaviors (NAM, 2020). Examples of behaviors that are of concern are smoking, obesity, and excessive alcohol abuse, and some rural areas have experienced critical problems with opioid abuse, as was noted in the section on substance use. In addition to the typical health issues of children, adults, and older adults, rural areas have a higher rate of accidents due to the nature of agricultural work and work in factories in some areas as well as traffic accidents. Access to emergency services is important but may be limited. Obstetrical services are also inadequate in some locations. When needed services are limited, people must travel long distances to get the needed services, and this may lead to increased risk and further problems. Typical health services needed in rural areas are not much different from those needed in urban areas and include primary care, clinics (such as federally qualified health centers), emergency, pharmacy, obstetrics, pediatrics, oncology, substance use treatment, mental health, school health, environmental health (e.g., safety, clean water, air quality), home healthcare, and long-term care.

Social services are also required and should address SDOH related to the rural community. Racial and ethnic diversity is also present in rural areas due to the need for labor leading to an increased use of migrant workers, as discussed in other sections. This also has an impact on the health status of rural populations.

As these areas struggle with access to healthcare, one healthcare need that is affected is pharmacy access. A study conducted in 2018 noted the following (Salako et al., 2018):

- Over the past 16 years, 1,231 independently owned rural pharmacies (16.1%) in the United States have closed. The most drastic decline occurred between 2007 and 2009. This decline has continued through 2018, although at a slower rate.
- A total of 630 rural communities that had at least one retail (independent, chain, or franchise) pharmacy in March 2003 had no such pharmacy as of March 2018.

This type of loss makes it difficult for these communities to obtain routine necessary care as medications make up a part of this care.

With the increased use of telehealth, which has been further stimulated by COVID-19 and related health needs, rural areas have seen a rising need for telehealth access but often experience barriers to effective service, which limits health equity. One of the challenges is access to broadband services, which may be limited in some locations, as well as the cost of personal electronic equipment and lack of access to services. It is now recognized that telehealth can help in increasing access to health services; however, it must be effective and accessible. It will take some time to develop and expand these services.

Persons Who Experience Mental Health Problems

The CDC monitors data on mental health and emphasizes the following:

> Mental health is an important part of overall health and well-being. Mental health includes our emotional, psychological, and social well-being. It affects how we think, feel, and act. It also helps determine how we handle stress, relate to others, and make healthy choices. Mental health is important at every stage of life, from childhood and adolescence through adulthood."
> (HHS, CDC, 2021f)

This description indicates that people with mental health challenges comprise a vulnerable population, and mental health impacts all areas of the country as well as all socioeconomic and racial and ethnic groups. COVID-19 has had a major impact on the mental health of all people, causing anxiety, fear, depression, the loss of family and friends, isolation, changes to economic status, and general loss.

In 2021, the U.S. Surgeon General expressed concern about the impact of the COVID-19 pandemic on mental health. The office developed recommendations that individuals, families, community organizations, technology companies, governments, and others can take to improve the mental health of children, adolescents, and young adults (HHS, Office of the Surgeon General [OSG], 2021). He noted that there was a problem with increasing mental health concerns among young people before COVID, but now it is worse with increased feelings of helplessness, depression, and thoughts of suicide — and rates have increased over the past decade. To address these problems, *Protecting Youth Mental Health: The U.S. Surgeon General's Advisory* identifies the following recommendations (HHS, OSG, 2021):

- Recognize that mental health is an essential part of overall health.
- Empower youth and their families to recognize, manage, and learn from difficult emotions.
- Ensure that every child has access to high-quality, affordable, and culturally competent mental health care.
- Support the mental health of children and youth in educational, community, and childcare settings. Expand and support the early childhood and education workforce.
- Address the economic and social barriers that contribute to poor mental health for young people, families, and caregivers.
- Increase timely data collection and research to identify and respond to youth mental health needs more rapidly. This includes more research on the relationship between technology and youth mental health, and technology companies should be more transparent with data and algorithmic processes to enable this research.

Nursing has also expressed its concerns about these health problems. The American Academy of Nursing commented, "Mental health challenges impact approximately 20% of youth, yet nearly two-thirds receive no professional treatment. The dynamics underlying this service gap are complex, involving access issues, a health system infrastructure ill-suited to serve vulnerable youth, provider shortages and broad reaching stigma that dampens help-seeking behavior" (Delaney et al., 2018). Action is needed to improve prevention, access, and equity for this vulnerable population. When children and teens have mental health problems, they often carry them into adulthood, which impacts their overall health, mental health, family and peer relationships, school performance, and employment.

Rural areas, as discussed earlier in this content, represent a vulnerable population, and one of the areas of concern is mental health. Services are often limited in rural areas, as they have less qualified staff to provide these services. The opioid epidemic is also more of an issue in rural areas, which is discussed more in the substance use section. These two factors plus social isolation and economic problems have an impact on the higher suicide rate in rural areas (*American Journal of Nursing*, 2022).

HRSA supported a study on children and mental health that reports increasing problems for children (2016–2020 data). For example, in children ages 3–17, anxiety rose by 29%, and depression increased by 27%. It is important to note that this occurred prior to COVID-19. There is now even greater concern that the pandemic has increased these problems for children, who have been frightened and/or isolated from family and friends, have experienced losses, and have had major changes to their school experiences. Many families that have dealt with major economic challenges have had other difficulties with housing and social support, for example. Parents have experienced their own mental health problems, such as anxiety, depression and increasing substance use, in attempts to alleviate problems, impacting children of all ages. On March 1, 2022, President Biden's State of the Union address identified mental health as a serious problem and announced initiatives to address the growing problem for children and adults. The following is a description of the strategies proposed by the administration (The White House, 2022):

Strengthen System Capacity: More than one-third of Americans live in a mental health professional shortage area.

- Invest in proven programs that bring providers into behavioral health.
- Pilot new approaches to train a diverse group of paraprofessionals.
- Build a national certification program for peer specialists.
- Promote the mental well-being of our front-line health workforce.
- Launch the 988 crisis response line and strengthen community-based crisis response.
- Expand the availability of evidence-based community mental health services.
- Invest in research on new practice models.

Connect Americans to care: Fewer than half of Americans with mental health problems receive care.

- Expand and strengthen mental health care benefits.
- Integrate mental health and substance use treatment into primary care settings.

- Improve veterans' access to same-day mental health care.
- Expand access to telehealth and virtual mental health care options.
- Expand access to mental health support in schools, colleges, and universities.
- Embed and co-locate mental health and substance use providers into community-based settings.
- Increase navigation resources so that providers can be found when needed.

Support Americans by creating healthy environments: We cannot transform mental health solely through the healthcare system. We must also address the determinants of behavioral health, invest in community services, and foster a culture and environment that broadly promotes mental wellness and recovery. This crisis is not a medical one, but a societal one.

- Strengthen children's privacy and ban targeted advertising for children online.
- Institute stronger online protections for young people, including prioritizing safety by design standards and practices for online platforms, products, and services.
- Stop discriminatory algorithmic decision-making that limits opportunities for young Americans.
- Invest in research on social media's mental harms.
- Expand early childhood and school-based intervention services and supports (half of all mental disorders begin before age 14).
- Set students up for success.
- Increase mental health resources for justice-involved populations.
- Train social and human services professionals in basic mental health skills.

These strategies are connected to public and community health and require communities to examine their services based on their needs and improve services and access. Nurses should be involved in all aspects of these efforts. Nursing education needs to participate in expanding content and experiences for students to prepare nurses who can be active, effective healthcare providers and must increase the workforce that cares for this vulnerable population in communities. It is significant that President Biden notes that the United States is experiencing a national mental health crisis. Having a president announce this and direct HHS and other parts of the federal government to examine the problem and improve provides support to make changes.

Suicide and self-harm injuries are a major concern and affect the entire healthcare system, and this must become a focus of public and community health. Suicide is one of the 10 leading causes of death in the United States; nearly 46,000 people died from suicide in 2020 (HHS, CDC, 2022d). (Note that data are typically a year or two behind the current year, as it takes time to collect, analyze, and report results.) The CDC recommends the following strategies for communities to use to prevent suicide (HHS, CDC, 2022d):

- Strengthen financial supports (e.g., jobs, housing, other related SDOH needs).
- Strengthen access to and delivery of suicide care (e.g., increase the mental workforce, enhance insurance, and improve interventions).
- Create protective environments (e.g., reduce access to weapons, monitor excess alcohol and other substance use).
- Promote connectedness (e.g., reduce isolation, provide opportunity for peer social interactions).
- Teach coping and problem-solving skills (e.g., all ages, children and parents).
- Identify and support people at risk.
- Lessen harms and prevent future risk (e.g., follow-up care, surveillance).

Communities need to provide prevention services such as health education about suicide and depression for all ages and include key community members who may interact with persons at risk, such as healthcare staff, teachers, law enforcement, staff at social services agencies, and religious leaders. Screening and assessment should be part of the community plan, including active helplines. Routine suicide prevention training should be offered. Treatment services must be respectful, accessible, and combined with follow-up. Health equity is critical. Another crucial factor in addressing the problem of suicide is staff having high competency in responding to this problem. Recommendations can be made for strategies that are needed, but if staff are not prepared, then the approaches will not be effective. In a recent survey of staff, only one-third felt strongly that they were prepared to care for these patients (Haskell, 2021). Suicide screening and risk assessment should be included in education for all nurses and updated as needed. If nurses are prepared, they can make a difference in the outcome of this health problem in communities.

Healthy People 2030 includes the goal to "improve mental health with a focus on prevention, screening, assessment, and treatment of mental disorders and behavioral conditions" (HHS, ODPHP, 2021d). These problems can lead to physical challenges, which can affect mental health. SDOH have a major impact on mental health status for people of all ages and nationwide. All the vulnerable populations discussed in this content are at risk for mental disorders and behavioral conditions.

The Behavioral Risk Factor Surveillance System (BRFSS) is used to collect information on health risk behaviors, preventative practices, and healthcare access. BRFSS questions focus on number of recent mentally unhealthy days, anxiety and depressive disorders, mental illness and stigma, and psychological distress. Review the link below to learn more about the BRFSS. What information can you find? How might a community use this to address the needs of this vulnerable population?
Website: https://www.cdc.gov/brfss/index.html

Persons Who Experience Substance Use Disorder

Addiction is "a chronic, relapsing disorder characterized by compulsive drug seeking and use despite adverse consequences" (NIH, National Institute for Nursing Research [NIDA], 2020). It is also viewed as a brain disorder because it involves functional changes to brain circuits involved in reward, stress, and self-control, and the changes related to addiction may be long-term and cause death. SUD affects all areas of a person's life and increases the risk of many problems—physical, psychological, social, and economic. There is variation in the age groups it affects as well as diversity, and it can be found in all types of locations, including rural and urban.

There is a need for more evidence-based approaches to prevent and respond to SUD as well as for pain and harm reduction measures. Some communities struggle daily in dealing with their increase in substance use and overdoses, both of which affect all types of healthcare services, including primary care, clinics, school health, emergency services and transport, and hospitals. People who experience SUD undergo losses, including deaths and chronic drug use outcomes that cause problems in all areas of a person's life and carry a heavy burden for families. All SDOH need to be considered when assessing substance use risks and planning interventions to prevent SUD and provide treatment. As is true with other vulnerable populations, health equity is critical, and racial and ethnic disparities also exist.

Alcohol and drug use is considered a major public health problem that can lead to injuries, violence, crime, pregnancy (due to risky sexual behavior),

HIV and AIDS, and other diseases. Examples of the level of use in teens include the following (HHS, CDC, 2022e):

- A total of 15% of high school students reported having used select illicit or injection drugs (e.g., cocaine, inhalants, heroin, methamphetamines, hallucinogens, or ecstasy).
- A total of 14% of students reported misusing prescription opioids.

Assessment of a community's substance use problem is an important part of public and community health. When communities plan assessment of teen substance use, some of the risk factors that should be considered are (HHS, CDC, 2020d):

- Family history of substance use
- Favorable parental attitudes toward the behavior
- Inadequate parental monitoring
- Parental substance use
- Family rejection of sexual orientation or gender identity
- Association with delinquent or substance-using peers
- Lack of school connectedness
- Low academic achievement
- Childhood sexual abuse
- Mental health issues

Communities must assess the status of substance use within the community routinely and use the data to determine the level of the problem. Responses should then be targeted on the factors that are most relevant in a specific community. These interventions and programs should emphasize parental and/or family education and engagement, family support, parental disapproval of substance use and monitoring, and school interventions, such as student and staff education and assessment of students. Communities need to routinely monitor the following to assess current status:

- Motor vehicle accidents and other accidents, such as falls, fire, and drownings
- Negative youth interactions (e.g., fighting) at school, sport, and social events
- Violence (homicide, suicide and self-harm, sexual assault, and intimate partner violence) and family disputes
- Emergency department admissions for alcohol poisoning

These experiences may indicate an increasing substance use problem, or, if initiatives have been taken to address the problem, the data may provide an assessment of outcomes from interventions.

There are many health problems related to SUD that should be considered. For example, excessive substance use may have an impact on pregnancies and newborns and lead to miscarriage or fetal alcohol spectrum disorders, which have long-term health implications for children and their development. Substance use often affects acute and chronic health issues. Withdrawal is a medical problem and requires assessment, treatment, and emergency response, in acute situations. Examples of some areas of health concerns that may be chronic include problems associated with heart disease, the liver, the neurological system, and immunity. Mental health (e.g., anxiety, depression, anger control problems, and psychosis) is also a concern. Social problems may be present prior to substance use and are also affected by SUD, including relationships with family and significant others, school performance, employment, and issues related to housing and financial status.

The use of substances to control pain is prevalent in the United States. Many people who are now addicted to drugs began with pain medications and in situations in which these drugs (i.e., opioids) were improperly prescribed. Due to the increasing opioid epidemic, in 2016 the CDC developed a resource to reduce unsafe opioid prescribing, titled *Guideline for Prescribing Opioids for Chronic Pain* (Dowell et al., 2016). In 2021, researchers conducted a study to examine the impact of these guidelines (Townsend et al., 2021). The results indicated that by 2018, there had been positive changes that resulted in a 20% reduction in the number of patients receiving at least one opioid prescription. Even though these statistics were encouraging, the researchers questioned if the use of voluntary guidelines did enough to address the problem and believed that this query required further assessment.

Often people do not consider nicotine to be a drug, but it is. Smoking and secondhand smoke, vaping, and cannabis are experiences and drugs that can lead to health problems. It is important to address these issues early, with children and teens and in the community. This can be done in schools and public areas (e.g., in businesses and restaurants) by eliminating smoking in these areas, for example.

Illicit drug use usually declines after young adulthood, but nearly 1 million adults ages 65 and older have SUD (2018 data) (NIH, NIDA, 2020). Older adults are more likely to be given prescriptions for chronic health conditions, and some of these drugs may be addictive, which may put these individuals at greater risk for addiction. In addition, older adults may not always be careful about taking medications while at home (e.g., taking more than prescribed, forgetting when they took their last dose or how much). Mental health issues, such as anxiety and depression, may also affect the use of medications. Even cannabis is a drug that is now considered in some locations to have medical benefits and may be prescribed to older adults; however, the fact it is widely used and sometimes prescribed does not mean that its usage cannot lead to addiction. In general, older adults have fewer SUDs, but this rate has increased. As is known for many drugs, age increases response and may lead to side effects, and this also applies to drugs that may lead to addiction. Older adults may also turn to drugs to cope with social and psychological issues, such as retirement, the loss of a spouse, a change in their living situation, financial concerns, and increased isolation. The most common drug that causes problems for older adults is alcohol. Even if an older adult is not addicted to alcohol, this does not mean that its use might not lead to problems such as falls, affect chronic health problems, trigger an incompatible interaction with prescribed or unprescribed medications, or cause driving accidents, for example.

Substance use is influenced by many cultural and social issues as well as stress. The COVID-19 pandemic is an example of the "perfect storm" for increased SUD risk, either for first-time users or as an exacerbation of a longer-term problem. Alcohol is a substance that is often abused. To examine this issue, current data from 2019 to 2020 indicated that during the first year of the COVID-19 pandemic, alcohol consumption increased as more people used alcohol as a method to cope with stress (White et al., 2022). The rate of transplants due to alcohol-associated liver disease increased, which affected the organ transplant population and also points to an increased use of alcohol. Emergency departments experienced a rise in the number of patients experiencing alcohol withdrawal, and the number of deaths associated with alcohol also increased. A similar review of other substances that are often abused would most likely find similar results, and all such reviews should consider that these problems are often not fully reported. In addition, people may not seek help, and thus the problem may not be accurately assessed within a community.

> The United States opioid crisis brings into sharp focus the health inequities for persons dependent on opioids due to long-term use for chronic pain and persons with opioid use disorder (OUD). Disparate access to health-care services, however, is widespread for vulnerable populations like frail older adults, children, incarcerated individuals, and members of racial, ethnic and sexual minorities, groups for whom opioid use exacts a heavy burden. Stigma combined with few prevention services and limited access to healthcare for life-saving treatment are costly for the society and its citizens. Principles of social justice maintain that all people deserve the same rights and should have access to the same resources for safe and comprehensive pain management and substance abuse treatment. (Naegle et al., 2020, p. 678)

It is recognized that providing effective safe pain treatment to prevent addiction is critical. An example of an initiative to address this problem within communities and in primary care is the AHRQ team approach. Review the six building blocks used by this approach and the toolkit at the following link. How might you apply this to public and community health nursing?

Website: https://www.ahrq.gov/patient-safety/settings/ambulatory/improve/six-building-blocks.html

The White House recently made a national decision and announced its assessment about the critical need to reduce the rise in drug-related overdoses and deaths. Increased use of illicit fentanyl, fentanyl analogs, methamphetamine, and cocaine, often in combination or in adulterated forms, has made the epidemic worse (American Medical Association, 2022; White House, 2021). Drug policy priorities should now focus on ensuring racial equity and promoting harm-reduction efforts and include (White House, 2021):

- Expanding access to evidence-based treatment
- Advancing racial equity issues in the approach to drug policy
- Enhancing evidence-based harm reduction efforts
- Supporting evidence-based prevention efforts to reduce youth substance use
- Reducing the supply of illicit substances
- Advancing recovery-ready workplaces and expanding the addiction workforce
- Expanding access to recovery support services

Data on substance use and death related to its use are not positive (HHS, CDC, 2022e). The current statistics must also be viewed from the perspective of the COVID-19 pandemic, which has had an impact on the SUD vulnerable population. The following provides some information on the status of the problem (HHS, CDC, 2022e):

- The death rate connected to drug use was highest among Native Americans after the COVID-19 pandemic began. Black individuals experienced the greatest increase.
- U.S. drug overdose deaths were at another record high in 2020; more than 91,000 people died.
- There were rises in the number of drug overdose deaths among both men and women, in all racial and ethnic populations, and among all ages 15 and older.

- The data indicate that at the beginning of the pandemic, more people began to use drugs for first time. For example, in late June 2020, in a survey of 5,400 people, 13% reported they had started or increased their substance use to cope with the stress and emotions related to COVID-19.

The data include some information about the effect of COVID-19, but later data will provide a better description of its effect on substance use. It would be easy to assume that drug overdose deaths were more related to the experience of COVID-19; however, at this time, experts do not believe this is the case. Prior to the onset of COVID-19, the United States was experiencing a major drug epidemic, and the deaths were most likely part of the cycle of a great number of individuals having addiction problems. COVID-19 had an impact, as it increased isolation and therefore decreased access to treatment, for example, but it could not be identified as the sole cause of these deaths. This might change with later data.

Nursing has also increased its concern about the growing substance use problem from the perspective of nursing education and practice. "Because persons across the lifespan from the fetus to older adult (irrespective of gender, culture, ethnicity, and race) can be negatively affected by substance use, the American Academy of Nursing endorses the position that all nurses, across specialties and settings in which care is provided, must be able to competently and confidently identify persons who may be at risk because of substance use, prevent the progression to a diagnosable disorder, and support those in recovery from substance use" (Finnell & Mitchell, 2020, p. 683). More will need to be done to prepare nurses so that they can provide effective nursing care and participate in population health services for the population of people experiencing SUD.

Impact of Violence and Abuse on Vulnerable Populations and Communities

Many communities, including rural and urban, experience violence. This problem is difficult to ignore when it is reported in the news, and it includes individual, children, family, partner, group, workplace, and school violence. The following highlights some examples of violence representing a vulnerable population that affects many sectors across the age, diversity, and socioeconomic spectrums and in many communities. Even healthcare staff experience violence—from patients, family members, and even coworkers. In the latter case, the violence is often experienced as verbal abuse. The Joint Commission, the primary accrediting association for healthcare organizations, issued an alert about healthcare violence, thus acknowledging that this is a critical problem (2021). Violence is present in all communities, whether it is acknowledged or not.

> Motor vehicle crashes, homicide, domestic and school violence, child abuse and neglect, suicide, and unintentional drug overdoses are important public health concerns in the United States. In addition to their immediate health impact, the effects of injuries and violence extend well beyond the injured person or victim of violence, affecting family members, friends, coworkers, employers, and communities. Witnessing or being a victim of violence is linked to lifelong negative physical, emotional, and social consequences. Both unintentional injuries and those caused by acts of violence are among the top 15 killers of Americans of all ages. Injuries are the leading cause of death for Americans ages 1 to 44, and a leading cause of disability for all ages, regardless of sex, race and ethnicity, or socioeconomic status. Each year, more than 29 million people suffer an injury severe enough that emergency department treatment is needed. More than 180,000 people each year die from these injuries, with approximately 51,000 of these deaths resulting from a violent event. Many intentional and unintentional injuries are preventable. (HHS, ODPHP, 2022b)

Recognizing the importance of the growing problem of violence, Healthy People 2030 includes violence in its objectives with its goal to "prevent violence and related injuries and death" (HHS, ODPHP, 2022b).

Review the Healthy People 2030 objectives aimed at preventing violence at the link below. What are the categories used to identify the objectives? Select one category and examine the goals. What can you learn about them? Click on the objectives to obtain additional information. Consider the information. How does it relate to public and community health nursing?
Website: https://health.gov/healthypeople/objectives-and-data/browse-objectives/violence-prevention

The following subsections discuss specific examples of violence.

Child Abuse and Violence

Children of all ages experience abuse and violence. Infants and very young children also experience maltreatment and neglect by parents and others. Child abuse is any intentional violent or threatening maltreatment of a child, physical or psychological and includes sexual abuse. It is a preventable act. In 2020, there were 618,399 victims of child abuse, a rate that was lower than the previous year and the lowest since 2012 (Statista, 2022). Human trafficking is also a form of child abuse and is not uncommon in some areas of world. The risk for this danger increases when children experience radical changes and risk. For example, because there is a greater number of refugees from Ukraine who are children, there is concern that some of them may become involved in situations in which they might be abused in this way. The following are examples from the U.S. data on child abuse (HHS, CDC, 2021g):

- **Child abuse and neglect are common.** At least one in seven children have experienced child abuse and/or neglect in the past year, and this statistic is likely an underestimate. In 2019, 1,840 children in the United States died due to abuse and neglect.
- **Children living in poverty experience more abuse and neglect.** Experiencing poverty can place a lot of stress on families, which may increase the risk for child abuse and neglect. The rate of child abuse and neglect is five times higher for children in families with lower socioeconomic status than children in families with higher socioeconomic status.
- **Child maltreatment is costly.** In the United States, the total lifetime economic burden associated with child abuse and neglect was approximately $428 billion in 2015. This economic burden rivals the cost of other high-profile public health problems, such as stroke and Type 2 diabetes.

Bullying

Bullying has become a serious violence problem for children of all ages. The term *bullying* describes aggressive behavior that may be done one on one or by groups and may be face to face or via the Internet (i.e., cyberbullying). Bullying can result in physical injury, emotional distress, and social stress, which affect family, peer relationships, academic performance, and feeling unsafe in the home environment. In 2020, one in five high school students reported bullying at school, and one in six high school students reported being cyberbullied. Fourteen percent of high schools reported bullying as a discipline problem (HHS, CDC, 2021h). Prevention and intervention are typically the responsibility of parents, family members, and school staff. However, all healthcare and social services staff and those who interact with children and teens in a variety of settings (e.g., sports, social, and community activities) should be alert to bullying and recognize it as violence. Prevention should include providing safe places for children and teens, using open communication, and being alert to the use of technology through which cyberbullying can easily go unnoticed. Assessment—particularly being alert to anxiety, depression, and anger—is critical and should be followed by using effective interventions. It's common to also focus on the victim, but these steps should also apply to working with children and teens who may use bullying as a coping mechanism. For both the victim and anyone who is using bullying, it is important to identify and understand the factors that increase the risk of the behavior, including stress, mental health problems, family stress, limited social skills, concern about physical appearance, economic issues such as poverty, and problems regarding diversity, equity, race, and ethnicity, among others. Bullying can have a long-term impact on health, both physical and psychological, and can lead to further violence and the use of substances such as alcohol and drugs.

Gun Violence

Adults, children, and teens are at risk for gun violence. The United States has experienced a rising number of gun incidents. For example, school shootings continue, with the majority being children causing the violence. This leads to injuries and death as well as major trauma for all children and school staff and the families involved. Another common situation of gun violence is in neighborhoods. In this case, the violence can be one on one, group- or gang-related, connected to other crimes (e.g., robbery and assault), or accidental—someone is in the wrong place at the wrong time. Gun violence related to domestic disputes, family problems, and suicide is also a problem. The phenomenon may also be caused by the accidental use of a gun; for example, a child finds a parent's gun, and the gun fires. It is critical that gun safety includes issues related to storage and security because access to weapons increases not only this type of gun violence risk but also the opportunity for someone to obtain and then intentionally use a gun. Communities need greater monitoring of access and must provide routine gun safety education to their citizens. If a family has a gun, the children involved should also be included in this education. Gun violence is a problem found in urban areas and suburbs as well as rural communities. No area is exempt. It is also costly as many gun injuries require complex healthcare.

Intimate Partner Violence

Intimate partner violence (IPV) is a serious public health concern. IPV is abuse or aggression in a romantic relationship, which may or may not be with a spouse. The typical types of behavior include (HHS, CDC, 2021i):

- **Physical violence,** which is when a person hurts or tries to hurt a partner by hitting, kicking, or using another type of physical force

- **Sexual violence,** which is when a person is forcing or attempting to force a partner to take part in a sex act, sexual touching, or a nonphysical sexual event (e.g., sexting) when the latter does not or cannot consent
- **Stalking,** which is a pattern of repeated, unwanted attention and contact by a partner that causes fear or concern for one's own safety or that of someone close to the victim
- **Psychological aggression,** which is the use of verbal and nonverbal communication with the intent to harm another partner, either mentally or emotionally, and/or to exert control over another partner

It is important for communities to recognize that IVP is not a minor problem and not uncommon, as an estimated one in four women and nearly one in 10 men have experienced sexual violence, physical violence, and/or stalking by an intimate partner during their lifetime.

"The Centers for Disease Control and Prevention estimates that one in five women in the United States experience severe intimate-partner violence over the course of their lifetimes, resulting in physical injuries, most commonly to the head, neck and face. Concussions are likely to appear with alarming regularity" (HHS, CDC, 2021i). The latter can lead to chronic brain injuries that may not be immediately recognized but that later cause symptoms such as headaches and memory issues, which are indications similar to those experienced by some football players with head injuries. IVP experiences impact individuals' physical and mental well-being over a lifetime and may interfere with relationships, family, and work.

Healthcare Staff Violence

Healthcare staff members are a vulnerable population for violence. In a survey of more than 6,000 nurses conducted by the American Nurses Association from 2019 to 2020, 23% indicated that they had experienced verbal or nonverbal aggression from a person of authority. Thirty-one percent experienced verbal or nonverbal aggression from a peer, and 35% surveyed experienced verbal and/or physical threats from a patient or patient's family member (The Joint Commission, 2022). As is true for most data on violence, not all incidents are reported, and thus the statistics regarding this violence are most likely lower than the actual number of experiences.

Healthcare staff violence and bullying have increased during the past few years. This violence can be verbal and/or physical and may result in injury or even death. Sources of the violence include patients, families or significant others, other staff, personal such as staff family member, and individuals who seem disconnected from the staff or healthcare services. This problem has become so severe that The Joint Commission issued a requirement for its accredited organizations to implement a workplace-focused violence prevention program that must include a reporting system, data review, incident follow-up, and employee training (Stand, 2022).

A work environment in which staff feel they are at risk for violence has a negative impact on all aspects of healthcare delivery. It can interfere with safe, high-quality care; for example, this type of stress may lead to errors, missed care, and miscommunication, among other issues. Teamwork is negatively affected, which interferes with effective and efficient work. The risk of violence can lead to healthcare problems for the staff, such as physical problems that may develop and psychological reactions, including anxiety and depression. These responses may lead to time off from work, staffing issues, and, in some cases, workers leaving their positions. Violence may also cause staff to experience unsafe behaviors and situations, such as use of substances (e.g., alcohol and drugs), smoking, automobile accidents due to stress and fatigue, and family and personal relationship problems.

Population Health Policy and Interventions

This section examines several issues that are important in supporting effective population health. Local, state, and national policies influence all aspects of population health and outcomes. Access, quality, and outcomes are critical elements to consider in health policy and are important in population health management and measurement. Funding and costs are always concerns, including payment for health services and availability and type of health insurance, the lack of which may require the use of personal funds or the inability to pay bills. Several examples of major population health policies, programs, and interventions are described below.

Population Health Policy

Population health policy is important to understand as it guides decisions about healthcare services. Nurses also must be directly involved in the development, implementation, and evaluation of these policies and advocate for effective, efficient services. There are grave challenges in providing population health service, such as funding limitations and rising costs, aging populations with greater and more complex needs, workforce shortages and the need for improved competencies, health equity and health disparities concerns, and the impact of SDOH on health outcomes. Principles of population health policy connect population health to public health and preventive medicine. Policies are directives, plans, and courses of action required by law (Bhattacharya & Bhatt, 2017). Policy development needs to consider early detection, treatment, mitigation, and rehabilitation. Political, economic, epidemiological, ethical, behavioral, and legal factors influence the development of these polices. Policymakers should also recognize the heterogeneity of population health needs among various groups with different demographics and in a variety of locations. Individual rights must be considered to support health equity and social justice. Policy evaluation is an important aspect of development. Population health management should be aligned with organizational strategic planning and human resources planning and apply effective population measurement.

HHS recognizes the importance of population health in many of its activities, including the major responsibilities assigned to the CDC. HHS with CDC activities:

> views population health as an interdisciplinary, customizable approach that allows health departments to connect practice to policy for change to happen locally. This approach utilizes non-traditional partnerships among different sectors of the community—public health, industry, academia, health care, local government entities, etc.—to achieve positive health outcomes. Population health brings significant health concerns into focus and addresses ways that resources can be allocated to overcome the problems that drive poor health conditions in the population. (HHS, CDC, 2020e)

This HHS's viewpoint has an impact on policies that are related to health and social needs.

The CDC's Division of Population Health (DPH) is focused on the supporting and developing population health. The purpose of this division is to improve the nation's health by providing state and local data on chronic diseases, risk factors, and outcomes. DPH activities include prevention strategies for specific populations and settings, support and facilitation of the development and use of innovative public health programs, and data analytics. In addition, this division of the CDC is engaged in prevention research to better ensure evidence-based practices in population health (HHS, CDC, DPH, 2021).

Access, Quality, and Outcomes

Access, quality, and outcomes are critical aspects of all healthcare delivery; however, most healthcare providers tend to focus more on their implications on acute care. Public and community health must also consider access, quality, and outcomes, and this includes implications for population health.

Quality improvement is a major issue in acute healthcare delivery today; however, it is not enough to consider solely hospital care if healthcare delivery is to improve in all settings for all people. There is no single agency or organization that is responsible for the improvement of population health overall. The only way to accomplish this objective is through collaboration and coordination among a variety of agencies and organizations, community service providers, the private sector, and other relevant stakeholders. The goal is to improve the health of every person and population within communities through planning and coordinating to ensure measurement, innovation, collaboration, and improvement to achieve the **Triple Aim** goals of better care, smarter spending, and healthier people and communities (HHS, CMS, 2021b). See **Figure 3**.

In examining population health policy, one aspect that is reviewed is the overall national health status. One method used for assessment is a comparison of outcome data with similar-income countries, although no two

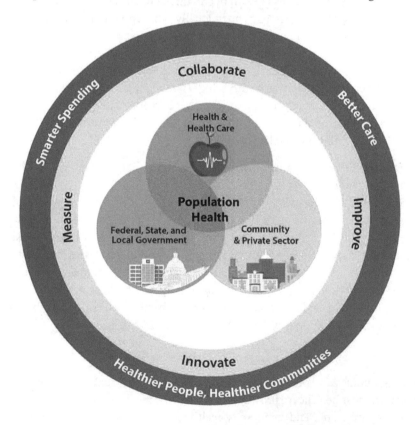

Figure 3.   Population Health Measures. Source: https://www.cms.gov/files/document/blueprint-population-health-measures.pdf.

countries are alike in their health systems. We also know that the United States does not have universal health coverage, whereas many developed countries do. One study was conducted that compared 11 high-income countries and focused on access to care, care process, administrative efficiency, equity, and healthcare outcomes (Schneider et al., 2021). The Commonwealth Fund was involved in this study. The key findings were as follows:

1. The top-performing countries overall were Norway, the Netherlands, and Australia.
2. The United States ranked last overall, despite spending far more of its gross domestic product on health care.
3. The United States also ranked last on access to care, administrative efficiency, equity, and healthcare outcomes but second on measures of care process.

It is clear this is a critical report, and the results indicate that the United States needs to improve its healthcare. A question that is important and examined in this study was, what were the differences in the high-ranking countries compared to the United States? Several differences that are important to consider in improving U.S. healthcare were identified. The higher-ranking countries used the universal coverage model, thus reducing costs for individuals; they provided primary care, viewing it as high-value services that should be equitable for people in all communities; administrative procedures were efficient, providing more time and funds for improvement; and more social services were provided for children and working-age adults. Each of these variances represent areas that should be developed and improved in the United States. The study also concluded by noting that there were two healthcare systems in the United States, one for people with finances and insurance that provided access to regular care and another for people without sufficient income and insurance. In addition, it is noted that the United States ranked in last place in seven of the Commonwealth Fund studies since 2004. This weakness in the healthcare system is particularly difficult for vulnerable populations, whose needs go unmet and become complex and who are also negatively affected by the SDOH.

Uninsured and Underinsured

The preliminary estimates about U.S. health insurance for the first six months of 2021 indicate that 9.6% of U.S. residents, or 31.1 million people, lacked health insurance when surveyed in the first six months of 2021 (HHS, CDC, NCHS, 2021a). This statistic is similar to the uninsured rate for 2020. The CDC data for various population groups indicate the following (HHS, CDC, NCHS, 2021a):

- Among children, 4.4% were uninsured, 44.7% had public coverage, and 53.1% had private coverage.
- Among adults younger than age 65, Hispanic adults (31.4%) were more likely than Black (14.7%), White (9.0%), and Asian (6.1%) adults to be uninsured.
- The percentage of people younger than age 65 with exchange-based coverage increased from 3.7% in 2019 to 4.3%.

The passing of the Affordable Care Act of 2010 (ACA) has led to a reduction in the number of uninsured individuals by providing other options for insurance, and Medicare and Medicaid offer coverage to many vulnerable populations. Despite these efforts to increase health insurance access, the United States still has a high rate of people who are uninsured.

In addition to problems with uninsurance, there are many people who do not have enough insurance for their needs. They are considered underinsured, as they cannot afford to pay for all the costs for their health services even though they have health insurance. Medical debt is a real problem for many in the United States. It is most likely that COVID-19 will increase this problem.

> Government data estimates that 9% of adults—or roughly 23 million people—owe more than $250 due to health costs. About half of those reporting significant medical debt owe more than $2,000. A small share (representing about 1 percent of all adults) owes more than $10,000, and the group accounts for the vast majority of all medical debt owed by people in the U.S. (Rae et al., 2022)

Medical debt has implications for housing and personal belongings as well as the ability to pay other bills and provide for basic needs such as food. It also may limit transportation options. We know that during the COVID-19 pandemic, many people lost work time or their jobs, and salaries were reduced, and these factors affect health coverage and increases bills. All of this adds to stress and health problems, both physical and psychological, and may cause family and social challenges and increase issues related to substance use and violence, for example.

View the short video on the ACA. What information is provided? How does this apply to nursing?
Website: https://www.hhs.gov/healthcare/about-the-aca/index.html

Examples of Major Population Policies, Programs, and Interventions

In 2021, the HHS and the OSG released *Community Health and Economic Prosperity: Engaging Businesses as Stewards and Stakeholders—A Report of the Surgeon General.* This was the first time the federal government had prepared a report like this one.

> With the onset of COVID-19, the U.S. has faced new, additional challenges to health and disruptions to the economy. "We know that economic opportunity—as well as the stable families, healthy environments, and strong communities it supports—is good for health. But too many Americans are born into and grow up in low-opportunity neighborhoods. This creates costs for business and for society, as so many Americans never achieve their potential in the workforce, are unable to reach independence, and see their health and the health of their loved ones suffer as a result," said HHS Secretary Alex M. Azar. This Surgeon General's report offers a way forward for the United States to recover from the COVID-19 pandemic and to build a healthier, more prosperous future for all Americans. (HHS, 2021b)

The report explains why it is important for business leaders to care about community health and asks for active involvement of business leaders to build healthier communities and an improved economy for all, emphasizing that community health is connected to economic prosperity. Health policies need to include all relevant stakeholders, and communities that want to improve population health must develop collaborations within their communities. This report emphasizes that business leaders need to be included as well. The following content provides examples of major population policies, programs, and interventions.

The HHS and the HRSA provided an update on the one-year anniversary of the American Rescue Plan that described its activities. Review the information. What are the major issues addressed and some of the HRSA activities? How does this information relate to this content's information?

Website: https://www.hrsa.gov/about/news/press-releases/american-rescue-plan-one-year-anniversary

Disease Prevention and Health Promotion for Vulnerable Populations

Disease prevention and **health promotion** are critical interventions for all, but they are particularly important for vulnerable populations who may not have easy access to routine care and prevention. In addition, health promotion requires healthy living habits, such as healthy nutrition, exercise, stress reduction, clean air and water, and safe living conditions. Racial and ethnic disparities are factors that need to be considered when these services are offered, and in some situations, disparities have occurred. In addition, health insurance or coverage of costs for preventive services may be required and may be limited for some. The ACA increased access to preventive services for people who did not have these benefits prior to the legislation, such as screenings for specific health conditions. Another factor important in health promotion and disease prevention is that even when access is possible, many people do not follow through on prevention and health promotion, which results in gaps in preventive services utilization and racial/ethnic disparities (Abdus, 2021).

The ODPHP, which is part of HHS, "encourages all Americans to lead healthy and active lives. We accomplish this by establishing and promoting national public health priorities, translating science into policy, guidance, and tools, and working to improve health literacy and equitable access to clear and actionable health information" (HHS, ODPHP, 2021e). The ODPHP manages major national health initiatives such as Healthy People 2030, Healthy Aging, and Health Literacy.

Review information about ODPHP initiatives.
Healthy People 2030: See **Appendix B**.
Healthy Aging: https://health.gov/news/tag/healthy-aging
Health Literacy: https://health.gov/our-work/national-health-initiatives/health-literacy

Disease prevention focuses on stopping disease before it develops as well as reducing risk of disease progression and complications. There are three levels of disease prevention applied in healthcare, as detailed below:

- **Primary prevention:** Applies interventions to stop disease from occurring. This level includes health promotion. Examples include immunizations, health education on healthy eating and exercise, and community places for exercise. The focus is on improving the health of the population.

- **Secondary prevention:** Applies interventions and screening to reduce disease progression and complications using early detection. Screening such as for cancer and hypertension are commonly used in communities in healthcare settings and even offered at sites in the community, such as during fairs, in malls/shopping centers, and at schools.
- **Tertiary prevention:** Applies interventions when there are disabilities from disease and the goal is to maintain and, when possible, improve functioning. Examples include providing diabetes education and insulin and rehabilitation after a stroke or a serious injury.

The U.S. Preventive Services Task Force (USPSTF) emphasizes the need for shared decision-making (SDM), which "should not be judged on whether it produces better health outcomes. Rather, it is the ethical right of patients to be provided with information and to make decisions collaboratively with their clinician" (USPSTF, 2022). It is best that health decisions are based on evidence that is shared and understood. SDM can help reduce inequities in preventive services.

Health promotion focuses on interventions that support healthy lifestyles and safe environments, which are a part of primary prevention. Communities are involved in health promotion, as demonstrated by many of the public health essential services. See **Appendix A** for more information on these services. Public health nursing is engaged in these activities serving the needs of populations, such as health teaching, advocacy, case management, surveillance, participation in public health policy development and implementation, monitoring of health outcomes, and the development and implementation of health service programs.

Health Literacy

Health literacy is an important factor that affects population health and vulnerable populations. Individuals need to understand health information and its implications as well participate actively in health decisions (i.e., SDM), but this also applies to populations. Vulnerable populations may experience even greater barriers to effective health literacy due to such factors as language barriers and lack of education, technology access, or access to healthcare providers for questions. The following are definitions of the two health literacy perspectives (HHS, CDC, 2021d):

- **Personal health literacy** is the degree to which individuals can find, understand, and use information and services to inform health-related decisions and actions for themselves and others.

- **Organizational health literacy** is the degree to which organizations equitably enable individuals to find, understand, and use information and services to inform health-related decisions and actions for themselves and others.

These definitions emphasize that people need to not only understand health information but also use information and make well-informed decisions. There needs to be concern about health literacy not only for individuals and acute care but also for populations and in public and community care. All types of healthcare organizations (acute care, public, and community health) must address health literacy within their structure, policies, and activities. The government (local, state, and federal) needs to incorporate health literacy considerations in policies and legislation, resources provided to healthcare providers, funding, and research.

Health literacy affects health outcomes and disparities. For example, if an individual does not understand the importance of taking medications or instructions about use, this will impact their health outcomes. Problems with health literacy also affect underutilization of prevention and health promotion. However, we need to know more about the relationship of health literacy to health disparities in vulnerable populations that may have special characteristics and needs that influence effective health literacy. Communities need to consider at-risk populations and barriers that limit their health literacy and then use this information to improve health literacy.

Health literacy is a central focus of Healthy People 2030 and was included in the previous version (2020). One of the overarching goals focuses on health literacy—"Eliminate health disparities, achieve health equity, and attain health literacy to improve the health and well-being of all"—and includes six objectives (HHS, ODPHP, 2021f):

- Increase the proportion of adults whose healthcare provider checked their understanding.
- Decrease the proportion of adults who report poor communication with their healthcare provider.
- Increase the proportion of adults whose healthcare providers involved them in decisions as much as the individuals wanted.
- Increase the proportion of people who say their online medical record is easy to understand.
- Increase the proportion of adults with limited English proficiency who say their providers explain things clearly.
- Increase the health literacy of the population.

The inclusion of these goals in Healthy People 2030 increases opportunities to monitor progress, improve health literacy, and reduce health disparities in population health. **Appendix C** identifies several reports about health literacy that have been published.

Health **misinformation** is a problem within the health system, particularly in public and community health, and is associated with health literacy. This fact was demonstrated during the COVID-19 pandemic and caused barriers to effective use of prevention measures, such as immunization and use of masks, social distancing, and quarantining. Misinformation is false, incomplete, or inaccurate information and may be shared intentionally or unintentionally. Typically, this information is shared easily and quickly, and with today's dependence on electronic communication, there is little that can stop the spread once it begins. Misinformation can cause harm to individuals, families, populations, and communities. The U.S. Surgeon General's office expressed concern about this problem and offered resources to reduce misinformation (HHS, OSG, 2022).

The Health Literate Care Model is part of the ODPHP Health Literacy initiative and encourages the use of a universal precaution, emphasizing that effective health literacy requires the following (HHS, ODPHP, 2021f):

- Approach all patients as if they are at risk of not understanding health information.
- Employ a range of strategies for clear communication.
- Confirm that patients understand what providers are saying.

Nurses should be familiar with and apply this model.

Review the Health Literate Care Model described at the link. Who are the community partners? What strategies should be used by health-literate organizations? What are the elements to improve outcomes?
Website: https://health.gov/sites/default/files/2019-10/HLCM_09-16_508.pdf

Healthy People 2030

The HHS, its agencies, and other government departments are responsible for assessing and developing plans and resources to ensure the health of all people who live in the United States—to promote health and prevent disease and illness. HHS works with healthcare services at the federal, state, and local levels. As part of this responsibility, Healthy People 2030 is a major federal initiative that provides a comprehensive plan focused on health promotion and disease prevention and routinely assesses national health status. The initiative is reviewed and updated every 10 years, with five past editions

(1979, 1990, 2000, 2010, 2020) and the current edition due to end in 2030. The latest version's vision and major goals focus on the topics of health conditions, health behaviors, populations, settings and systems, and SDOH. Throughout this content, there are references to Healthy People 2030 on population health, vulnerable populations, and the initiative's application to health services and outcomes. See **Appendix B** for more information about Healthy People 2030.

National Healthcare Quality and Disparities Report

For 19 years the HHS, through its agency the AHRQ, maintains the U.S. system to monitor health status and publishes an annual report of health quality and disparities, titled *National Healthcare Quality and Disparities Report* (NHQDR). The report was initially a report on quality, and later a second report was initiated on disparities. The two reports have since been combined into one after it was recognized that disparities are related to the quality of care and vice versa. The monitoring process includes measures focused on access to care, affordable care, care coordination, effective treatment, healthy living, patient safety, and person-centered care (HHS, AHRQ, 2022). The report presents in chart form with an analysis the latest available findings on healthcare quality and access and identifies disparities related to race and ethnicity, income, and other SDOH.

The 2021 NHQDR offers information on some of the vulnerable populations discussed in the content. Review information on aging (older adults), children and adolescents, and health literacy.
Website: https://nhqrnet.ahrq.gov/inhqrdr/reports/factsheets

CDC Population Health Initiatives

The CDC Population Health and Healthcare Office (PHHO) assists and collaborates with public health professionals to ensure there are evidence-based policies to guide public health initiatives. The PHHO initiative Health Impact in 5 Years (HI-5) focuses on) nonclinical, communitywide approaches that have evidence reporting 1) positive health impacts, 2) results within five years, and 3) cost-effectiveness and/or cost savings over the lifetime of the population or earlier (CDC, PHHO, 2022). SDOH are recognized as important, as is the need to make healthy choices easier. **Figure** 4 describes HI-5. The base of the pyramid in the figure focuses on interventions that will have the greatest impact because they address needs of entire populations.

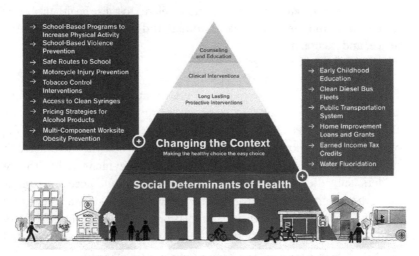

Figure 4.   Health Impact in 5 Years (HI-5). Source: https://www.cdc.gov/policy/hst/hi5/index.html.

The following is a list of problems that HI-5 interventions can help prevent or reduce:

- Anxiety and depression
- Asthma
- Blood pressure
- Bronchitis
- Cancer
- Cardiovascular disease
- Child abuse and neglect
- Cognitive development
- Infant mortality
- Liver cirrhosis
- Motor vehicle injuries
- Obesity
- Dental caries
- Pneumonia
- Sexually transmittable infections
- Sexual violence
- Teenage pregnancy
- Traumatic brain injury
- Type 2 diabetes
- Youth violence

Earlier content on vulnerable populations relates to these health problems (e.g., children and teens, pregnant women and newborns, older adults, violence, and mental health).

HRSA Special Initiatives for Vulnerable Populations

HRSA activities focus on expanding healthcare access and resources in underserved populations. In 2022, HRSA announced funding for its initiative Promoting Pediatric Primary Prevention Challenge. This financing provided $66.5 million to support community-based vaccine outreach efforts, more than $560 million in pandemic relief payments to healthcare providers, subsidies to increase virtual care quality and access, and new funding to support primary care residency programs. Children and teens are a vulnerable population, and their health has been affected by the COVID-19 experience, along with their continued need for routine healthcare expected for this population.

Other funding has also been announced focused on additional services to improve health outcomes in underserved communities, promote health equity, and support the health workforce, such as training physicians and nurses for underserved and rural areas, expanding vaccination outreach for COVID-19, increasing the number of pediatric routine vaccinations and well-child visits, expanding virtual healthcare access and quality through community health centers, and supporting maintenance of access to essential primary care services (HHS, HRSA, 2022a).

In addition, the 2022 HRSA initiative for healthcare workforce training provided additional funds for the primary care workforce and was supported by the National Health Service Corps (NHSC). The NHSC works to build healthy communities and uses a network of providers, residents, and students. Seventeen million people receive services through NHSC and its nearly 20,000 providers, which not only expands the healthcare workforce but also improves rural and mental and behavioral healthcare services (HHS, HRSA, NHS, 2022). The NHSC's services are not well known to the public outside of the areas where they are provided, but they are critical to vulnerable populations in high-need areas and health professional shortage areas.

An important HRSA-supported program is the community health center model. Community health centers are community-based and patient-centered and provide comprehensive, culturally competent, high-quality primary healthcare services to vulnerable populations, such as people experiencing homelessness, agricultural workers, residents of public housing, and veterans (HHS, HRSA, 2021b). These centers provide easier access to pharmacy, mental health, SUD, and oral health services. They are offered in locations that typically experience economic, geographic, and/or cultural barriers. The centers' goal is to increase access to affordable quality care that is sensitive to health equity and reduces disparities. Community health centers emphasize coordinated case management and have access to health information technology and other updated approaches to healthcare. HRSA's goals for community health centers are as follows (HHS, HRSA, 2021b):

- Deliver comprehensive, culturally competent, high-quality primary healthcare, as well as supportive services, such as health education, translation, and transportation.
- Provide services regardless of patients' ability to pay and charge for services on a sliding fee scale.
- Develop systems of patient-centered and integrated care that respond to the unique needs of diverse medically underserved areas and populations.
- Private nonprofit or public entities, including tribal and faith-based organizations, that operate under the direction of a patient-majority governing board.
- Meet requirements regarding administrative, clinical, and financial operations.

The centers receive federal funding, and sometimes the financing is directed toward centers that focus on a specific vulnerable underserved population, such as individuals and families experiencing homelessness, migratory and seasonal agricultural workers, and residents of public housing.

HRSA's strategic plan for 2019–2022 includes the following goals (HHS, HRSA, 2019, p. 3):

1. Improve access to quality healthcare and services.
2. Foster a healthcare workforce able to address current and emerging needs.
3. Enhance population health and address health disparities through community partnerships.
4. Maximize the value and impact of HRSA programs.
5. Optimize HRSA operations to enhance efficiency, effectiveness, innovation, and accountability.

These objectives are important and relevant to this content, but Goal 3 is particularly important as it focuses on population health. HRSA aims to "increase access to health care and improve health outcomes for vulnerable populations by enhancing community partnerships with entities from diverse geographic areas, groups needing or offering particular health care services, professional organizations, and others that support the populations HRSA serves" (HHA, HRSA, 2019, p. 10).

Research and Vulnerable Populations

Evidence-based practice (EBP) is an important aspect of healthcare delivery and nursing. Typically, the focus of EBP is on acute care; however, EBP is also needed for population health and to improve care for vulnerable populations. An example of the recognition of the need for evidence and further research is the work done by the USPSTF, which is required to submit a report annually to the U.S. Congress that identifies gaps in scientific evidence and recommendations for more research related to clinical preventive services (HHS, AHRQ, USPSTF, 2021). The report is an important source and driver for research and the expansion of EBP. The initiative recognizes disparities in health due to factors such as age, race, ethnicity, sex and gender, sexual orientation, and social risk factors. The 2021 report indicated research gaps related to health equity in cardiovascular disease and cancer prevention, and this type of information should in the future be considered in plans for population health.

Nursing Roles and Interventions in Population Health

Population health is part of nursing practice. The American Association of Colleges of Nursing (AACN) includes population health as a domain in its nursing education standards and emphasizes prevention and disease management of populations and the need for public health collaboration (AACN, 2021).

Nursing and Population Health

Due to its recognition of the importance of population health and nurses, the Robert Wood Johnson Foundation (RWFJ) published a report on this topic, titled *Nursing Education and the Path to Population Health Improvement* (RWJF, 2019). Based on this report, the RWJF developed a two-phase nursing project. The first, which has been completed (RWJF, 2019), focused on Population Health in Nursing (PHIN 1) to explore promising models of nursing education and practice related to improving population health. The second phase, PHIN 2, concentrates on describing current and emerging nursing roles in population health practice and how nurses should be prepared for these roles. The first phase results identified PHIN core content and competencies as related to epidemiology/biostatistics, SDOH, health equity, interprofessional teamwork, healthcare economics, and systems thinking. Important education methods identified for this content and role were case studies and simulation, intentional and structured academic-practice partnerships, interprofessional education, and service learning. Challenges exist in providing population health content and experiences in nursing education. The top three challenges are the need for faculty expertise in population health, the lack of availability of clinical experiences to meet the goals, and the necessity of faculty support that reflects acceptance of population health as an important part of the curriculum. Structured metrics are needed to evaluate student outcomes and then improve learning experiences necessary to develop population health competency in the nursing workforce. It is important that population health be integrated throughout the curriculum to encourage all students to view it as a critical part of the healthcare continuum. Additional work is now being done to improve nursing education based on these results. In addition, the second phase of the project, which focuses on practice in population health, is in process to examine required population health competencies, develop strategies to improve population health, and further develop initiatives in practice. See **Appendix A** for more information on public health competencies and **Appendix C** for information on some of the key NAM reports that focus on population health and related education.

Community health needs assessment is "the process of collecting, analyzing, and interpreting quantitative or qualitative data on health outcomes and health correlates and determinants; the identification of health disparities or resources that can be used to address priority health needs" (HHS, HRSA, 2019, p. 16). Nurses should be leading assessment programs for all populations. They understand the need for assessment and the assessment process; however, support services are needed to provide effective population health assessment, such as technology to collect and analyze data. Communities need structured methods for ensuring that community health assessment occurs. This information is critical for understanding a community's health status and identifying its vulnerable populations and their needs. This step then leads to planning, implementation, and evaluation of outcomes. Nurses must work with interprofessional teams and a variety of stakeholders, including local and state government and staff, healthcare organizations (e.g., clinics, hospitals, school health, occupational health, home healthcare agencies, long-term care facilities), all specialty areas, businesses, religious leaders, and community social organizations. Nurse advocacy should be part of the movement, and nurses should serve as leaders to improve care, health equity, and reduce disparities and include care for vulnerable populations (Lal, 2020).

As was noted in an earlier section, there is need for research in population health, and nursing should be also engaged in this research. EBP in public and community health requires current evidence addressing the many needs and problems that require interventions. This will also have an impact on improving care and health outcomes. Health equity and disparities are important aspects to include in this research. These topics are included in the draft 2022–2026 National Institute for Nursing Research (NINR) strategic plan, which is scheduled to be approved in 2022 (NIH, NINR, 2022).

Barriers to Providing Care in Communities

Involvement in public and community health programs for populations is not easy. There are many barriers to success. It takes time to achieve outcomes, and outcome evaluation requires a system (e.g., identification of types of data needed, data collection, analysis and interpretation). There is a need for qualified staff, and evaluation should include healthcare professionals, community leaders and staff, technological staff, budget and finance, and other relevant stakeholders. Funding is critical and always a barrier—the amount and sources. Engaging representatives from local and state nursing organizations as well as academic nursing can help to provide additional expertise and hands-on assistance; for example, nursing students (undergraduate and graduate) can assist in data collection, planning, implementation, and evaluation. Nurses may also volunteer to participate in community health initiatives—such as serving at a community fair to screen for hypertension, on a disaster planning committee, or as a volunteer during a flood disaster to assess needs and provide health services.

As mentioned in the section on health literacy, misinformation is a problem in public and community health and has been a major issue during the COVID-19 pandemic. Nurses have a key role in sharing health information—providing accurate timely information, listening to people to appreciate understanding, and identifying and correcting misinformation. The HHS now has initiatives to reduce misinformation. Review the link and explain how nurses in school health, occupational health, and community clinics might use this type of tool. Select one of the vulnerable populations in the content and describe how the tool might be applied to the needs of the population.
   Website: https://www.hhs.gov/sites/default/files/talk-to-your-community-about-health-misinformation-english.pdf

Nursing Leadership to Improve and Maintain Population Health

Accomplishing health equity within a community must be a joint effort—a collaboration and partnership with the community's health organizations, such as the hospital(s) and public and community health services as well as social services. Nurses need to assume leadership roles in these efforts. For example, the AHA recognizes the need for this partnership and offers resources to help develop collaboration through its Institute for Diversity and Health Equity (IFDHE; AHA, IFDHE, 2021). Nurses have many roles in acute care, and one responsibility in which nurse leaders should engage is working with their colleagues in public and community health and vice versa to ensure that all who need health services receive them where and when they are needed. For example, when hospitals initiate collaborations to meet the AHA IFDHE program standards, nurses should be included from the hospital and public and community health, as should local academic nurses. **Appendix C** includes information on the report *The Future of Nursing 2020–2030: Charting a Path to Achieve Health Equity*, which emphasizes the importance of nurses in health equity and population health (National Academy of Medicine, 2021b).

Summary

The nation's health depends on effective population health that integrates health equity and aims to reduce disparities that exist for many within the diverse environment. This content presented views of population health and the need to apply population health management and measurement to ensure positive health outcomes. In addition to access to healthcare services, health is influenced by many factors—including those related to families and culture, social, housing, environment, the justice system, education, employment, religion, and others. Nurses must be involved in population health and consider population health management in nursing practice. The profession recognizes that this is important, and we need more activity within the profession to lead efforts to improve health for the many vulnerable populations, some of whom were discussed in this content. Nurses have much to offer public and community health due to their expertise. Population health is not a new concept but has gained greater relevance. A key question posed in 2014—yet still not answered—by Kindig and Isham is as follows: "What is the optimal balance of investments (e.g., dollars, time, policies) in the multiple determinants of health (e.g., behavior, environment, socioeconomic status, medical care, genetics) over the life course that will maximize overall health outcomes and minimize health inequities at the population level?" (Kindig, 2022). This is a complex research and policy question. Nurses should be involved in finding answers as they will eventually impact the profession and nursing practice.

Discussion Questions

1. How does population health relate to nursing care? Provide three examples.
2. Select one of the vulnerable populations described in the content and explain the implications of SDOH, health equity, and disparities for the population you have identified.
3. If you had a choice to practice nursing with any of the vulnerable populations described in this content, which population would you choose? What is your rationale for your choice?
4. You have been asked by a someone who is beginning the nursing education program about the difference in acute care nursing and public and community health nursing. To provide an answer, make a list of pros and cons to acute care nursing practice and public and community health nursing.

References

AARP. (2022). *Paid family leave: States with workplace laws to help parents and caregivers.* https://www.aarp.org/caregiving/financial-legal/info-2019/paid-family-leave-laws.html

Abdus, S. (2021). Trends in differences across subgroups of adults in preventive utilization. *Medical Care, 59*(12), 1059–1066.

American Association of Colleges of Nursing. (2021). *The essentials: Core competencies for professional nursing education.* https://www.aacnnursing.org/Portals/42/Academic Nursing/pdf/Essentials-2021.pdf

American Hospital Association. (2020). *Pathways to population health: An invitation to health care change agents.* https://www.aha.org/system/files/media/file/2020/09/Pathways-to-Population-Health-Framework.pdf

American Hospital Association. (2022). *AHA population health framework.* https://www.aha.org/center/population-health-fundamentals

American Hospital Association, AHA Institute for Diversity and Health Equity. (2021). *Community partnerships: Strategies to accelerate health equity.* https://ifdhe.aha.org/system/files/media/file/2021/08/ifdhe_community_partnership_toolkit.pdf

American Journal of Nursing. (2022). Mental health services under strain in rural America. *American Journal of Nursing, 122*(2), 13.

American Medical Association. (2021). *2022 national drug control strategy.* https://searchlf.ama-assn.org/letter/documentDownload?uri=%2Funstructured%2Fbinary%2Fletter%2FLETTERS%2F2021-7-9-Letter-to-LaBelle-re-ONDCP-2022-Strategy-v2.pdf

American Public Health Association. (2021a). *Social justice and health*. https://www.apha.org/what-is-public-health/generation-public-health/our-work/social-justice

American Public Health Association. (2021b). *Creating the healthiest nation: Opportunity youth*. https://www.apha.org/-/media/Files/PDF/topics/equity/Opportunity_Youth.ashx

Auld, M. E., Allen, M. P., Hampton, H., et al. (2020). Health literacy and health education in schools: Collaboration for action. *NAM Perspectives*. Discussion paper. National Academy of Medicine. Washington, DC. https://doi.org/10.31478/202007b

Baily, Z. D., Feldman, J. M., & Bassett, M. T. (2021). How structural racism works— Racist policies as a root cause of U.S. racial health inequities. *New England Journal of Medicine, 384*, 768–773.

Barlow, J. (2015). *Vulnerable mothers in pregnancy and postnatal period*. Nursing in Practice. https://www.nursinginpractice.com/clinical/vulnerable-mothers-in-pregnancy-and-the-postnatal-period/

Bhattacharya, D., & Bhatt, J. (2017). Seven foundational principles of population health policy. *Population Health Management, 20*(5), 383–388.https://repository.usfca.edu/cgi/viewcontent.cgi?article=1131&context=nursing_fac

Callahan, E. A., Vafiadis, D. K., Cameraon, K. A., & Stanford, F. C. (2022). A call for solutions for healthy aging through a systems-based, equitable approach to obesity. *Journal of the American Geriatrics Society*. https://agsjournals.onlinelibrary.wiley.com/doi/full/10.1111/jgs.17732

Centers for Disease Control and Prevention, Population Health and Healthcare Office. (2022). *Population health and healthcare*. https://www.cdc.gov/policy/phho/index.html

De Biasi, A., Wolfe, M., Carmody, J., Fulter, T., & Auerbach, J. (2020). Creating an age-friendly public health system. *Innovative Aging, 4*(1), igz044. https://pubmed.ncbi.nlm.nih.gov/32405542/

Delaney, K. R., Burke, P., DeSocio, J., Greenberg, C. S., & Sharp, D. (2018). Building mental health and caring for vulnerable children: Increasing prevention, access, and equity. *Nursing Outlook, 66*, 590–593. https://doi.org/10.1016/j.outlook.2018.10.004

Dowell, D., Haegerich, T. M., & Chou, R. (2016). CDC guideline for prescribing opioids for chronic pain—United States, 2016. *MMWR Weekly Report, 65*(1), 1–49. http://dx.doi.org/10.15585/mmwr.rr6501e1

Finnell, D., & Mitchell, A. (2020). The crucial role of all current and future nurses in addressing the continuum of substance use. *Nursing Outlook, 68*, 682–684.

GBD (Global Burden of Disease) 2015 Maternal Mortality Collaborators. (2016). Global, regional, and national levels of Maternal Mortality, 1990–2015: A systematic analysis for the Global Burden of Disease Study 2015. *The Lancet, 388*, P1775–P1812.

Gooch, K., Gonzalez, G., & Jensik, L. (2022). *50 states of population health*. Becker's Hospital Review. https://www.beckershospitalreview.com/50-states-of-population-health/50-states-of-population-health.html?origin=BHRSUN&utm_source=BHRSUN&utm_medium=email&utm_content=newsletter&oly_enc_id=2271D2140545A3G

Haskell, B. (2021). Suicide assessment and follow-up care. *American Nurse Journal, 16*(12), 23–26.

Healthgrades. (2020). *Top 10 children's health concerns.* https://www.healthgrades.com/right-care/childrens-health/top-10-childrens-health-concerns

Institute for Healthcare Improvement. (2022). *Age-friendly health systems exceeds scale and impact goals to improve care for older adults.* http://www.ihi.org/about/news/Documents/IHIPressRelease_AFHSMilestone_March2022.pdf?utm_campaign=tw&utm_medium=email&_hsmi=205942714&_hsenc=p2ANqtz-8XG2SPP2wcwhigUMBCFoh_K_utGsAjbZhO2vneHWtrpmC2O6RUKfvUtCYz6Q9gMgbWkYn3fho2x4XKP_WOYV9l_v0PBg&utm_content=205823048&utm_source=hs_email

Keisler-Starkey, K., & Bunch, L. N. (2021). *Health insurance coverage in the United States: 2020.* Report number P60-274. U.S. Census Bureau. https://www.census.gov/library/publications/2021/demo/p60-274.html

Kindig, D., & Stoddart, G. (2003). What is population health? *American Journal of Public Health, 93*(3), 380–383.

Kindig, D. (2022). *The promise of population health: A scenario for the next two decades.* Commentary, National Academy of Medicine. https://doi.org/10.31478/202203a

Kindig, D. A., & Isham, G. (2014). Population health improvement: A community health business model that engages partners in all sectors. *Frontiers of Health Services Management, 30*(4), 3–20.

Kiser, T., & Hulton, L. (2018). Addressing health care needs in the homeless population: A new approach using participatory action research. *SAGE Open, 8*(3). https://journals.sagepub.com/doi/full/10.1177/2158244018789750

Krubiner, C., & Faden, R. (2017). Pregnant women should not be categorized as a vulnerable population in biomedical research studies: Ending a vicious cycle of vulnerability. *Journal of Medical Ethics, 43*(10), 664–665.

Lal, M. (2020). Innovative nurse-led initiatives improve population health. *JONA: The Journal of Nursing Administration, 50*(2), 59–60.

Lewis, N. (2014). *Populations, population health, and the evolution of population management: Making sense of terminology in U.S. healthcare today.* http://www.ihi.org/communities/blogs/population-health-population-management-terminology-in-us-health-care

Liu, M., & Hwang, S. (2021). Healthcare for homeless people. *Nature Reviews Disease Primer, 7,* 5. https://www.nature.com/articles/s41572-020-00241-2

Naegle, M. A., Finnell, D. S., Kaplan, L., et al. (2020). Opioid crisis through the lens of social justice. *Nursing Outlook, 68*(5), P678–P681. https://doi.org/10.1016/j.outlook.2020.08.014

National Association of Community Health Centers. (2016). *Population health management.* http://www.nachc.org/wp-content/uploads/2015/12/NACHC_pophealth_factsheet_FINAL.pdf

National Academy of Medicine. (2021a). *Population health in rural America in 2020: Proceedings of a workshop.* National Academies Press.

National Academy of Medicine. (2021b). *The future of nursing 2020–2030: Charting a path to achieving health equity.* National Academies Press.

National Academy of Medicine. (2022a). *Reducing inequalities between lesbian, gay, bisexual, transgender, and queer adolescents and cisgender, heterosexual adolescents: Proceedings of a workshop.* National Academies Press.

National Academy of Medicine. (2022b). *Realizing the promise of equity in the organ transplantation system.* National Academies Press.

National Association of Community Health Centers. (2016). *Population health management.* http://www.nachc.org/wp-content/uploads/2015/12/NACHC_pophealth_factsheet_FINAL.pdf

National Committee for Quality Assurance, Healthcare Effectiveness Data and Information Set. (2019). *Population health management: Roadmap for integrated delivery networks.* https://www.ncqa.org/wp-content/uploads/2019/11/20191216_PHM_Roadmap.pdf

National Health Care for the Homeless Council. (2019). *Homelessness and health: What's the connection?* https://nhchc.org/wp-content/uploads/2019/08/homelessness-and-health.pdf

National Institutes of Health, National Center Institute. (2022). *Immunosuppressed.* https://www.cancer.gov/publications/dictionaries/cancer-terms/def/immunosuppressed

National Institutes of Health, National Institute for Nursing Research. (2022). *NINR strategic plan (2022–2026)—Under development.* https://www.ninr.nih.gov/aboutninr/ninr-mission-and-strategic-plan

National Institutes of Health, National Institute on Drug Abuse. (2020). *What is drug addiction?* https://nida.nih.gov/publications/drugs-brains-behavior-science-addiction/drug-misuse-addiction#:~:text=Addiction%20is%20defined%20as%20a,and%20use%20despite%20adverse%20consequences

Omerov, P., Craftman, A. G., Mattsson, E., & Klarare, A. (2019). Homeless persons' experiences of health- and social care: A systematic integrative review. *Health & Social Care in the Community, 28*(1), 1–11.

Rae, M., Claxton, G., Amin, K., et al. (2022). *The burden of medical debt in the United States.* https://www.kff.org/health-costs/issue-brief/the-burden-of-medical-debt-in-the-united-states/

Robert Wood Johnson Foundation. (2019). *Nursing education and the path to population health improvement.* https://campaignforaction.org/wp-content/uploads/2019/03/NursingEducationPathtoHealthImprovement.pdf

Robert Wood Johnson Foundation. (2022). *Systemic racism and health equity.* https://www.rwjf.org/en/library/collections/racism-and-health.html

Rountree, J., Hess, N., & Lyke, A. (2019). *Health conditions among unsheltered adults in the U.S.* California Policy Lab. https://www.capolicylab.org/wp-content/uploads/2019/10/Health-Conditions-Among-Unsheltered-Adults-in-the-U.S.pdf

Salako, A., Ulrich, F., & Mueller, K. J. (2018). Update: Independently owned pharmacy closures in rural America, 2003–2018. *Rural Policy Brief, 2,* 1–6. https://pubmed.ncbi.nlm.nih.gov/30080364/

Schneider, E., Shah, A., Doty, M. M., Tikkanen, R., Fields, K., & Williams, R. D. II. (2021). *Mirror, mirror 2021: Reflecting poorly. Health care in the U.S. compared to other high-income countries.* The Commonwealth Fund. https://www.commonwealthfund.org/publications/fund-reports/2021/aug/mirror-mirror-2021-reflecting-poorly

Semega, J., Kollar, M., Creamer, J., & Mohanty, A. (2019). *Income and poverty in the United States: 2018.* U.S. Census Bureau. https://www.census.gov/content/dam/Census/library/publications/2019/demo/p60-266.pdf

Shaunna, C., Boss, L., & Lynn, M. (2020). The relationship between food insecurity and cost-related medication nonadherence in older adults: A systematic review. *American Journal of Nursing, 120*(6), 24–36.

Statista. (2022). *Total number of victims of child abuse in the United States from 2012 to 2020.* https://www.statista.com/statistics/639375/number-of-child-abuse-cases-in-the-us/

Stiefel, M., & Nolan, K. (2012). *A guide to measuring the Triple Aim: Population health, experience of care, and per capita cost.* Institute for Healthcare Improvement Innovation Series white paper. Institute for Healthcare Improvement. http://www.ihi.org/resources/Pages/IHIWhitePapers/AGuidetoMeasuringTripleAim.aspx

The Joint Commission. (2021). *Sentinel Alert 59: Physical and verbal violence against health care workers.* https://www.jointcommission.org/resources/patient-safety-topics/sentinel-event/sentinel-event-alert-newsletters/sentinel-event-alert-59-physical-and-verbal-violence-against-health-care-workers/

The Joint Commission. (2022). Workplace prevention resources. https://www.jointcommission.org/resources/patient-safety-topics/workplace-violence-prevention/

Townsend, T., Cerdá, M., Bohnert, A., Lagisetty, P., & Haffajee, R. L. (2021). CDC guideline for opioid prescribing associated with reduced dispensing to certain patients with chronic pain. *HealthAffairs, 40*(11), 1766–1775. https://doi.org/10.1377/hlthaff.2021.00135

UNHCR. (2022). *What is a refugee?* https://www.unhcr.org/what-is-a-refugee.html

U.S. Department of Health and Human Services. (2021a). *Biden-Harris administration begins distributing American Rescue Plan rural funding to support providers impacted by pandemic.* https://www.hhs.gov/about/news/2021/11/23/biden-admin-begins-distributing-arp-prf-support-to-providers-impacted-by-pandemic.html

U.S. Department of Health and Human Services. (2021b). *Community health and economic prosperity: Engaging businesses as stewards and stakeholders—A report of the Surgeon General.* https://www.hhs.gov/sites/default/files/chep-sgr-full-report.pdf

U.S. Department of Health and Human Services, Agency for Healthcare Quality and Research. (2021). *2019 National Healthcare Quality and Disparities Report.* https://www.ahrq.gov/research/findings/nhqrdr/nhqdr19/index.html

U.S. Department of Health and Human Services, Agency for Healthcare Quality and Research. (2022). *National Healthcare Quality and Disparities Reports.* https://www.ahrq.gov/research/findings/nhqrdr/index.html

U.S. Department of Health and Human Services, Agency for Healthcare Quality and Research, U.S. Preventive Task Force Services. (2021). Annual reports. https://www.uspreventiveservicestaskforce.org/uspstf/about-uspstf/reports-congress

U.S. Department of Health and Human Services, Centers for Disease Control and Prevention. (2017). *Health disparities.* https://www.cdc.gov/aging/disparities/index.htm

U.S. Department of Health and Human Services, Centers for Disease Control and Prevention. (2019a). *Transplant safety: Key facts.* https://www.cdc.gov/transplantsafety/overview/key-facts.html

U.S. Department of Health and Human Services, Centers for Disease Control and Prevention. (2019b). *Transplant safety.* https://www.cdc.gov/transplantsafety/index.html

U.S. Department of Health and Human Services, Centers for Disease Control and Prevention. (2020a). *Disability impacts all of us.* https://www.cdc.gov/ncbddd/disabilityandhealth/infographic-disability-impacts-all.html

U.S. Department of Health and Human Services, Centers for Disease Control and Prevention. (2020b). *Including people with disabilities in public health programs and activities.* https://www.cdc.gov/ncbddd/disabilityandhealth/disability-public-health.html

U.S. Department of Health and Human Services, Centers for Disease Control and Prevention. (2020c). *National health education standards.* https://www.cdc.gov/healthyschools/sher/standards/index.htm

U.S. Department of Health and Human Services, Centers for Disease Control and Prevention. (2020d). *High-risk substance use among youth.* https://www.cdc.gov/healthyyouth/substance-use/index.htm

U.S. Department of Health and Human Services, Centers for Disease Control and Prevention. (2020e). *What is population health?* https://www.cdc.gov/pophealthtraining/whatis.html

U.S. Department of Health and Human Services, Centers for Disease Control and Prevention. (2021a). *Introduction to public health.* https://www.cdc.gov/training/publichealth101/index.html

U.S. Department of Health and Human Services, Centers for Disease Control and Prevention. (2021b). *About chronic diseases.* https://www.cdc.gov/chronicdisease/about/index.htm

U.S. Department of Health and Human Services, Centers for Disease Control and Prevention. (2021c). *Lesbian, gay, bisexual, and transgender health.* https://www.cdc.gov/lgbthealth/index.htm

U.S. Department of Health and Human Services, Centers for Disease Control and Prevention. (2021d). *Racism and health.* https://www.cdc.gov/healthequity/racism-disparities/index.html

U.S. Department of Health and Human Services, Centers for Disease Control and Prevention. (2021e). *Immigrant, refugee, and migrant health.* https://www.cdc.gov/immigrantrefugeehealth/index.html

U.S. Department of Health and Human Services, Centers for Disease Control and Prevention. (2021f). *Mental health.* https://www.cdc.gov/mentalhealth/index.htm

U.S. Department of Health and Human Services, Centers for Disease Control and Prevention. (2021g). *Fast facts: Preventing child abuse & neglect.* https://www.cdc.gov/violenceprevention/childabuseandneglect/fastfact.html

U.S. Department of Health and Human Services, Centers for Disease Control and Prevention. (2021h). *Fast fact: Preventing bullying.* https://www.cdc.gov/violenceprevention/youthviolence/bullyingresearch/fastfact.html

U.S. Department of Health and Human Services, Centers for Disease Control and Prevention. (2021i). *Fast facts: Preventing intimate partner violence.* https://www.cdc.gov/violenceprevention/intimatepartnerviolence/fastfact.html

U.S. Department of Health and Human Services, Centers for Disease Control and Prevention. (2022a). *Health equity considerations and racial and ethnic minority groups.* https://www.cdc.gov/coronavirus/2019-ncov/community/health-equity/race-ethnicity.html

U.S. Department of Health and Human Services, Centers for Disease Control and Prevention. (2022b). *Populations and vulnerabilities.* https://www.cdc.gov/nceh/tracking/topics/PopulationsVulnerabilities.htm

U.S. Department of Health and Human Services, Centers for Disease Control and Prevention. (2022c). *Community health and economic prosperity* (CHEP). https://www.cdc.gov/policy/chep/index.html

U.S. Department of Health and Human Services, Centers for Disease Control and Prevention. (2022d). *Facts about suicide.* https://www.cdc.gov/suicide/facts/index.html

U.S. Department of Health and Human Services, Centers for Disease Control and Prevention. (2022e). *Illicit drug use.* https://www.cdc.gov/nchs/fastats/drug-use-illicit.htm

U.S. Department of Health and Human Services, Centers for Disease Control and Prevention, Division of Population Health. (2021). *Population health.* https://www.cdc.gov/populationhealth/index.html

U.S. Department of Health and Human Services, Centers for Disease Control and Prevention, National Center for Health Statistics. (2021a). *Health insurance coverage: Early release of estimates from the National Health Interview Survey, January-June 2021.* https://www.cdc.gov/nchs/data/nhis/earlyrelease/insur202111.pdf

U.S. Department of Health and Human Services, Centers for Disease Control and Prevention, National Center for Health Statistics. (2022). *Older persons' health*. https://www.cdc.gov/nchs/fastats/older-american-health.htm

U.S. Department of Health and Human Services, Centers for Disease Control and Prevention, Office of Minority Health. (2021). *Minority health social vulnerability index fact sheet*. https://onemap.cdc.gov/Portal/apps/MapSeries/index.html?appid=3384875c46d649ee9b452913fd64e3c4

U.S. Department of Health and Human Services, Centers for Disease Control and Prevention, Office of Minority Health & Health Equity. (2021). *Racism is a serious threat to public health*. https://www.cdc.gov/healthequity/racism-disparities/index.html

U.S. Department of Health and Human Services, Centers for Medicare & Medicaid Services. (2021a). *Health coverage options for Afghan evacuees*. https://www.medicaid.gov/medicaid/eligibility/downloads/hlth-cov-option-afghan-evac-fact-sheet.pdf

U.S. Department of Health and Human Services, Centers for Medicare & Medicaid Services. (2021b). *Population health measures*. https://www.cms.gov/files/document/blueprint-population-health-measures.pdf

U.S. Department of Health and Human Services, Health Resources & Services Administration. (2019). *Vision: Healthy communities, healthy people. 2019–2022 strategic plan*. https://www.hrsa.gov/sites/default/files/hrsa/about/strategic-plan/HRSA-strategic-plan-2019-2022.pdf

U.S. Department of Health and Human Services, Health Resources & Services Administration. (2021a). *National survey of children's health*. https://mchb.hrsa.gov/sites/default/files/mchb/data-research/national-survey-childrens-health-2021-overview-fact-sheet.pdf

U.S. Department of Health and Human Services, Health Resources & Services Administration. (2021b). *What is a health center?* https://bphc.hrsa.gov/about/what-is-a-health-center/index.html

U.S. Department of Health and Human Services, Health Resources & Services Administration. (2022). *HRSA works to expand health care access and resources in underserved populations*. https://www.hrsa.gov/about/news/press-releases/february-2022-roundup

U.S. Department of Health and Human Services, Health Resources & Services Administration, National Health Service Corps. (2022). *National Health Service Corps. About*. https://nhsc.hrsa.gov/about-us

U.S. Department of Health and Human Services, Office of Disease Prevention and Health Promotion. (2020). Healthy People 2030. https://health.gov/healthypeople/objectives-and-data/social-determinants-health

U.S. Department of Health and Human Services, Office of Disease Prevention and Health Promotion. (2021a). *Older adults*. Healthy People 2030. https://health.gov/healthypeople/objectives-and-data/browse-objectives/older-adults

U.S. Department of Health and Human Services, Office of Disease Prevention and Health Promotion. (2021b). *LGBT*. Healthy People 2030. https://health.gov/healthypeople/objectives-and-data/browse-objectives/lgbt

U.S. Department of Health and Human Services, Office of Disease Prevention and Health Promotion. (2021c). *Social determinants of health*. Healthy People 2030. https://health.gov/healthypeople/objectives-and-data/social-determinants-health

U.S. Department of Health and Human Services, Office of Disease Prevention and Health Promotion. (2021d). *Mental health and mental disorders*. Healthy People 2030. https://health.gov/healthypeople/objectives-and-data/browse-objectives/mental-health-and-mental-disorders

U.S. Department of Health and Human Services, Office of Disease Prevention and Health Promotion. (2021e). *About ODPHP*. https://health.gov/about-odphp

U.S. Department of Health and Human Services, Office of Disease Prevention and Health Promotion. (2021f). *Health literate care model*. https://health.gov/our-work/national-health-initiatives/health-literacy/health-literate-care-model

U.S. Department of Health and Human Services, Office of Disease Prevention and Health Promotion. (2022a). *Pregnancy and childbirth*. Healthy People 2030. https://health.gov/healthypeople/objectives-and-data/browse-objectives/pregnancy-and-childbirth

U.S. Department of Health and Human Services, Office of Disease Prevention and Health Promotion. (2022b). *Injury and violence*. Healthy People 2030. https://www.healthypeople.gov/2020/leading-health-indicators/2020-lhi-topics/Injury-and-Violence?source=govdelivery&utm_medium=email&utm_source=govdelivery

U.S. Department of Housing and Urban Development, Office of Policy Development and Research. (2020). *The 2018 Annual Homeless Assessment Report (AHAR) to Congress: PART 2: Estimates of Homelessness in the United States*. https://www.huduser.gov/portal/datasets/ahar/2018-ahar-part-2-pit-estimates-of-homelessness-in-the-us.html

U.S. Department of Health and Human Services, Office of the Surgeon General. (2021). *U.S. Surgeon General issues advisory on youth mental health crisis further exposed by COVID-19 pandemic*. https://www.hhs.gov/about/news/2021/12/07/us-surgeon-general-issues-advisory-on-youth-mental-health-crisis-further-exposed-by-covid-19-pandemic.html?utm_campaign=enews20211216&utm_medium=email&utm_source=govdelivery

U.S. Department of Health and Human Services, Office of the Surgeon General. (2022). *Health misinformation reports and publications*. https://www.hhs.gov/surgeongeneral/reports-and-publications/health-misinformation/index.html

U.S. Preventive Services Task Force. (2022). Collaboration and shared decision-making between patients and clinicians in preventive health care decision and U.S. Preventive Services Task Force recommendations. *JAMA, 327*(12), 1171–1176. doi:10.1001/jama.2022.3267

White, A. M., Castle, I-J. P., Powell, P. A., Hingson, R. W., & Koob, G. F. (2022). Alcohol-related deaths during the COVID-19 pandemic. *JAMA*. Published online March

18, 2022. doi:10.1001/jama.2022.4308. https://jamanetwork.com/journals/jama/fullarticle/2790491

White House. (2021). *The Biden-Harris administration's statement of drug policy priorities for Year One.* https://www.whitehouse.gov/wp-content/uploads/2021/03/BidenHarris-Statement-of-Drug-Policy-Priorities-April-1.pdf

White House. (2022). *Fact sheet: President Biden to announce strategy to address our national mental health crisis, as part of unity agenda in his first State of the Union.* https://www.whitehouse.gov/briefing-room/statements-releases/2022/03/01/fact-sheet-president-biden-to-announce-strategy-to-address-our-national-mental-health-crisis-as-part-of-unity-agenda-in-his-first-state-of-the-union/

Wilson, C. (1920). The untitled field of public health. *Modern Medicine, 2,* 183–191.

Wolfe, M., De Biasi, A., Carmody, J., Fulmer, T., & Auerbach, J. (2021). Expanding public health practice to address older adult health and well-being. *Journal of Public Health Management Practice, 27*(5), E189–E196. https://doi.org/10.1097/phh.0000000000001238

World Health Organization. (2020). *Children: New threats to health.* https://www.who.int/news-room/fact-sheets/detail/children-new-threats-to-health

World Health Organization. (2021a). *Social determinants of health.* https://www.who.int/teams/social-determinants-of-health

World Health Organization. (2021b). *Aging: Ageism.* https://www.who.int/news-room/questions-and-answers/item/ageing-ageism

Wyatt, R., Laderman, M., Botwinick, L., Mate, K., & Whittington, J. (2016). *Achieving health equity: A guide for health care organizations.* Institute for Health Improvement white paper. http://www.ihi.org/resources/Pages/IHIWhitePapers/Achieving-Health-Equity.aspx

Appendix A

Reducing Confusion With Some Critical Terms

The following content provides some basic information and terminology related to public and community health.

Public and Community Health

Public health is the area of healthcare that focuses on prevention and control of disease and disability, with particular concern for groups (i.e., populations and communities). Healthy behaviors and wellness are important for public health. **Figure A.1** identifies the major core sciences that are associated with public health and used to meet its goals.

Community health focuses on providing comprehensive accessible services to a community to ensure health needs are met, considers social determinants of health that affect the community, and aims to reduce health disparities while supporting health equity. The latter aim involves an increased emphasis on advocacy and policy development and implementation to ensure a healthy community.

Who Does Public and Community Health Serve?

Within public and community health, various terms are used to identify those who need assistance. Examples of these terms include:

- *Individuals* (also *patients*, *clients*, and *consumers*)
- *Families*
- *Aggregates* or *populations*
- *Communities*

The public and community health focus is less on individuals and more on groups (e.g., families; populations, such as persons with heart disease; and communities).

Figure A.1   Public Health Core Sciences. Source: https://www.cdc.gov/training/publichealth101/documents/introduction-to-public-health.pdf.

Healthcare Providers

Healthcare providers are individuals and organizations providing health services. Examples of individuals are professionals such as physicians, registered nurses, pharmacists, social workers, and others (e.g., nutritionists, government health inspectors [food, business safety], health educators, community planners, epidemiologists, public policymakers, school health staff, community first responders). Healthcare organizations include acute care hospitals, clinics, community-based service agencies, home healthcare agencies, centers providing urgent care and emergency services, and pharmacies. In communities, health departments and their associated services, such as clinics and often school health, provide critical services to the community. Within business and industry, occupational health services offer support for employees and health education and prevention and have an impact on the overall health of the community.

Groups and Teams

In this guide, the term *team* is used rather than *group*. Within healthcare (e.g., acute care, community health, and public health), *team* is more commonly used; staff are members of teams in their workplaces. Students need to become familiar with this term, and to encourage this perspective, the guide refers to student *teams* rather than *groups*.

The Public Health Model

There are three public health core functions:

- **Assessment:** Relates to essential services 1–2
- **Policy development:** Relates to essential services 3–5
- **Assurance:** Relates to essential services 6–10

Nurses who work in public and community health are involved in each of the three core functions and the following 10 public health essential services:

1. Assess and monitor population health status, factors that influence health, and community needs and assets.
2. Investigate, diagnose, and address health problems and hazards affecting the population.
3. Communicate effectively to inform and educate people about health, factors that influence it, and how to improve it.
4. Strengthen, support, and mobilize communities and partnerships to improve health.
5. Create, champion, and implement policies, plans, and laws that impact health.
6. Utilize legal and regulatory actions designed to improve and protect the public's health.
7. Ensure an effective system that enables equitable access to the individual services and care needed to be healthy.
8. Build and support a diverse and skilled public health workforce
9. Improve and innovate public health functions through ongoing evaluation, research, and continuous quality improvement.
10. Build and maintain a strong organizational infrastructure for public health.

Figure A.2 describes the interrelationship between the core functions and essential services.

Centers for Disease Control and Prevention, Excerpts from "Essential Public Health Services (Revised, 2020)," 2020.

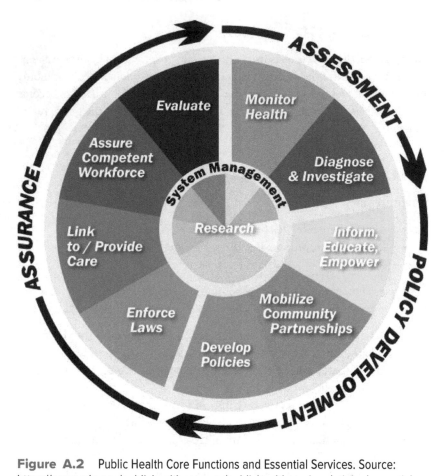

Figure A.2 Public Health Core Functions and Essential Services. Source: https://www.cdc.gov/publichealthgateway/publichealthservices/originalessential-healthservices.html.

Public Health Core Competencies

A collaborative of 24 national organizations concerned with public health education developed the following competencies. These are based on the 10 essential public health services and should be applied to all public health professionals. The goal of this collaboration is to improve public health by ensuring competent staff and effective healthcare organization performance. Identification of these competencies also recognizes the need for effective coordination and monitoring of outcomes among the key stakeholders in academic institutions, public health practice, and healthcare communities. Education must include not only preparation education but also ongoing staff education at the work site. The collaboration also notes that there is an ongoing need to develop effective strategies for positive public health outcomes. The following describes the domains—specific activity areas—emphasized in these core competencies:

Domain 1: Data Analytics and Assessment Skills

Focuses on factors that affect the health of the community, data collection, analysis of data, use of public health informatics applying data and information, assessment of community health status

Domain 2: Policy Development and Program Planning Skills

Development, implementation, and evaluation of policies, programs, and services to improve

Domain 3: Communication Skills

Strategies for internal and external use; responding to information, including misinformation and disinformation; facilitating individual, group, and organization communication

Domain 4: Health Equity Skills

Effective use of principles related to ethics, diversity, equity, inclusion, and justice; self-awareness of biases; working effectively in diverse situations and with diverse people to reduce systematic and structural barriers while advocating for health equity

Domain 5: Community Partnership Skills

Establishing community relationships and working to improve community health and resilience; collaborating and sharing power

Domain 6: Public Health Science Skills

With an understanding of systems, policies, and situations that impact public health, applying the 10 essential public health services, evidence-based practice, and support research to provide more evidence for public health practice

Domain 7: Management and Finance Skills

Effectively applying basic management and finance skills to public health, such as planning, quality, human resources, staff development, finance, policies, integration of diversity, teams and teamwork, collaboration, performance management, using the healthy community model, and application of three public health core functions and 10 essential services

Domain 8: Leadership and Systems-Thinking Skills

Identifies facilitators and barriers related to 10 essential public health services; serves as leader to encourage creativity, innovation, responding to current trends, directing effective change, collaborating with stakeholders in the community, and advocating for public health

Nurses must also follow relevant nursing standards and competencies.

Source: Council on Linkages Between Academia and Public Health Practice. (2021, October). *Core competencies for public health professionals.* http://www.phf.org/resourcestools/pages/core_public_health_competencies.aspx

The nursing profession responded to the development of the above public heath core competencies by aligning public health nursing competencies with them. The nursing competencies focus on public health nursing practice, from entry level to senior nursing management positions, and integrate the competencies that were developed for all public health professionals. There are also eight domains in the public health nursing competencies. Given that the focus in this guide is on health equity and disparities, domains that are particularly related to these issues are identified as follows, although many of the other domains are indirectly related to this content (Quad Council Coalition, 2018):

- **Cultural competency skills** focus on understanding and responding to diverse needs, assessing organizational cultural diversity and competence, assessing effects of policies and programs on various populations, and taking action to support a diverse public health workforce (relates to Domain 4).
- **Community dimensions of practice skills** focus on evaluating and developing linkages and relationships within the community, maintaining and advancing partnerships and community involvement,

negotiating for the use of community assets, defending public health policies and programs, and evaluating and improving the effectiveness of community engagement (relates to Domain 5).

Source: Quad Council Coalition. (2018). *Community/public health nursing [C/PHN] competencies.* https://www.cphno.org/wp-content/uploads/2020/08/QCC-C-PHN-COMPETENCIES-Approved_2018.05.04_Final-002.pdf

Public Health Nursing Standards

The American Nurses Association (ANA) has developed and updated standards for many specialties. *Public Health Nursing: Scope & Standards of Practice* includes standards related to the following: assessment, population diagnosis and priorities, outcomes identification, planning, implementation, coordination of care, health teaching and health promotion, consultation, prescriptive authority, regulatory activities, evaluation, professional performance for public health nursing, ethics, evidence-based practice and research, quality of practice, communication, leadership, collaboration, professional practice evaluation, resource utilization, environmental health, and advocacy. As is true for all ANA standards and as is mentioned in the guide's content, health equity is an important concern.

Source: American Nurses Association. (2013). *Public health nursing: Scope & standards of practice* (2nd ed.). https://www.nursingworld.org/nurses-books/public-health-nursing--scope--standards-of-practice-2nd-edition/" https://www.nursingworld.org/nurses-books/public-health-nursing--scope--standards-of-practice-2nd-edition/

References

American Nurses Association. (2013). *Public health nursing: Scope & standards of practice* (2nd ed.). https://www.nursingworld.org/nurses-books/public-health-nursing--scope--standards-of-practice-2nd-edition/

Council on Linkages Between Academia and Public Health Practice. (2021, October). *Core competencies for public health professionals.* http://www.phf.org/resourcestools/pages/core_public_health_competencies.aspx

Quad Council Coalition. (2018). *Community/public health nursing [C/PHN] competencies.* https://www.cphno.org/wp-content/uploads/2020/08/QCC-C-PHN-COMPETENCIES-Approved_2018.05.04_Final-002.pdf

Appendix B

The National Initiative to Improve the Nation's Health: Healthy People 2030

The U.S. Department of Health and Human Services (HHS), its agencies, and other government departments are responsible for assessing and developing plans and resources to ensure the health of all people who live in the United States by promoting health and preventing disease and illness. HHS works with healthcare services at the federal, state, and local levels. As part of this responsibility, Healthy People 2030 is a major federal program that provides a comprehensive plan focused on health promotion and disease prevention and routinely assesses national health status. The initiative is reviewed and updated every 10 years, with five past editions (1979, 1990, 2000, 2010, 2020, and the current edition, which is due to end in 2030). The latest version's vision and major goals focus on the topics of health conditions, health behaviors, populations, settings and systems, and social determinants of health (SDOH).

Health status is determined by measuring birth and death rates, life expectancy, quality of life, morbidity from specific diseases, risk factors, use of ambulatory care and inpatient care, accessibility to health providers and facilities, financing of healthcare services, health insurance coverage, access to healthcare, and other factors. Quality is a complex healthcare issue that affects the health status of individuals and communities. There is not one single factor or behavior that determines outcomes, but rather multiple factors—such as genetics, lifestyle, gender, race/ethnic factors, nutrition, poverty level, education, environment, injury, violence, environment, and unavailability or inaccessibility of quality health services.

Healthy People 2030 Framework

Vision

A society in which all people can achieve their full potential for health and well-being across the lifespan.

Mission

To promote, strengthen, and evaluate the nation's efforts to improve the health and well-being of all people.

Foundational Principles

Foundational principles explain the thinking that guides decisions about Healthy People 2030:

- Health and well-being of all people and communities are essential to a thriving, equitable society.
- Promoting health and well-being and preventing disease are linked efforts that encompass physical, mental, and social health dimensions.
- Investing to achieve the full potential for health and well-being for all provides valuable benefits to society.
- Achieving health and well-being requires eliminating health disparities, achieving health equity, and attaining health literacy.
- Healthy physical, social, and economic environments strengthen the potential to achieve health and well-being.
- Promoting and achieving the nation's health and well-being is a shared responsibility that is distributed across the national, state, tribal, and community levels, including the public, private, and not-for-profit sectors.
- Working to attain the full potential for health and well-being of the population is a component of decision-making and policy formulation across all sectors.

Overarching Goals

- Attain healthy, thriving lives and well-being, free of preventable disease, disability, injury, and premature death.
- Eliminate health disparities, achieve health equity, and attain health literacy to improve the health and well-being of all.

- Create social, physical, and economic environments that promote attaining full potential for health and well-being for all.
- Promote healthy development and healthy behaviors and well-being across all life stages.
- Engage leadership, key constituents, and the public across multiple sectors to take action and design policies that improve the health and well-being of all.

Plan of Action

To achieve the health and well-being of all people, relevant stakeholders need to be active partners, across the public, private, and nonprofit sectors. Healthy People conducts regular monitoring of the plan's progress. The results are made public on its website.

The Healthy People objectives are developed to meet the overall goals and are based on data and changed as needed during each 10-year cycle. This includes eight broad outcome measures used to assess the program's vision, 355 measurable core public health objectives with 10-year targets and related evidence-based interventions, developmental goals for public health issues with interventions, and research objectives directed at public health issues for which there are no evidence-based interventions.

Healthy People 2030 focuses on individual health and on communities. It describes a healthy community as one that maintains a high quality of life and is productive and safe, provides both treatment and prevention services to all community members, maintains necessary effective infrastructure (e.g., water, energy, roads, transportation, schools, playgrounds, and other services), and maintains a healthy environment (for example, issues of pollution, such as with air and water). Educational and community-based programs need to focus on preventing disease and injury, promoting and improving health, and enhancing quality of life. This view of a healthy community relates to the SDOH.

To meet Healthy People goals, community programs and services must provide broad access (e.g., located in schools, workplaces, healthcare facilities, and community sites) and offer prevention, monitoring, treatment, and rehabilitation services.

The Healthy People 2030 initiative not only provides a 10-year plan to improve healthcare in the United States but also monitors and reports on progress by assessing the outcome status of its goals and objectives. Data on current outcomes can be found on the Healthy People website. At the end of the 10-year period, all outcomes are evaluated and summarized. This

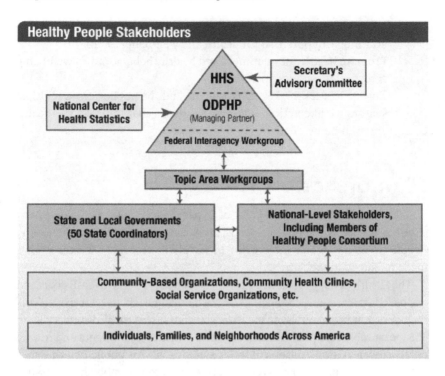

Figure B.1   Healthy People Stakeholders. Source: https://www.cdc.gov/nchs/about/factsheets/factsheet-hp2030.htm.

information is then used to develop the plan for the next 10 years—the goals, objectives, and leading indicators.

Stakeholders

Many organizations, government, and individuals are involved in the development, implementation, and evaluation of the Healthy People initiative. Nurses need to understand the importance of stakeholders so that they can collaborate with relevant stakeholders and advocate for healthy communities. **Figure B.1** describes the Healthy People stakeholders.

Healthy People 2030: Current Information

- Explore the leading health Indicators used by Healthy People to monitor its outcomes.

    Source: https://health.gov/healthypeople/objectives-and-data

- Explore SDOH and relationship to Healthy People.

  Source: https://health.gov/healthypeople/objectives-and-data

- Explore overall health and well-being measures.

  Source: https://health.gov/healthypeople/objectives-and-data

References

U.S. Department of Health and Human Services, Office of Disease Prevention and Health Promotion. (2021a). *Healthy People 2030.* https://health.gov/healthypeople" https://health.gov/healthypeople

U.S. Department of Health and Human Services, Office of Disease Prevention and Health Promotion. (2021b). *Tools for action*. Healthy People 2030. https://health.gov/healthypeople/tools-action" https://health.gov/healthypeople/tools-action

Appendix C

Institute of Medicine/National Academy of Medicine Reports

The National Academy of Medicine (NAM) is the former Institute of Medicine (IOM), and since 2015, it has been referred to as *NAM*. The IOM/NAM has provided significant examination of healthcare issues and expert advice to healthcare organizations, individual providers, and health policymakers, both governmental and nongovernmental (NAM, 2021). The IOM/NAM is a nongovernmental, nonprofit organization that was created in 1970. Why is it mentioned in this guide, which deals with equity and disparities? Its reports cover many topics, some of which are relevant to this content. The NAM asks experts to examine an issue, provides staff and funding for the review, and then publishes information from the review and often identifies recommendations (Finkelman, 2017). These recommendations are not laws or regulations, but they often have a major impact on healthcare decision-making.

The following are brief summaries of early reports that had a significant influence on how the nation's healthcare delivery system and health policy view quality care as well as more current reports that highlight some areas of interest to this guide's content. Some of the reports are mentioned within the guide's content.

To Err Is Human (1999) Due to growing questions about quality care, President William Clinton's Advisory Commission on Consumer Protection and Quality in the Health Care Industry stimulated further examination of quality and asked the IOM to further examine healthcare, focusing on errors. The report from this request, *To Err Is Human*, stirred a strong reaction by indicating that there were many errors in the U.S. healthcare system. The results were widely discussed in the media, so consumers became more aware of this problem. In addition, the report emphasized that the healthcare delivery system put too much emphasis on blame for errors, particularly on individual staff. This led to an active initiative to alter this approach.

Most errors are system errors, not individuals making mistakes. The report focused on acute care.

Crossing the Quality Chasm (2001) A second major report on healthcare quality followed *To Err Is Human*. It focused on broader issues of quality care and concluded that more information was needed. This report also focused on acute care. Even with President Clinton's commission's review and two extensive reviews and reports on healthcare quality, there was still concern that we did not know enough and the problem was extensive. Public and community health also needed to be examined, and later reports included this vital health care area.

Envisioning the National Healthcare Quality Report (2001) The 1999 and 2001 reports mentioned earlier identified the need for systematic monitoring of healthcare quality to better understand the status of quality care. This monitoring needed to be done routinely and include analysis and recommendations for improvement. *Envisioning the National Healthcare Quality Report* described an initial framework for the new annual monitoring process and report. The Agency for Healthcare Research and Quality, an agency within the U.S. Department of Health and Human Services, is responsible for this annual report (titled the *National Healthcare Quality and Disparities Report*), which initially focused solely on quality care.

Unequal Treatment: Confronting Racial and Ethnic Disparities in Health Care (2003) This report began to expand the healthcare perspective by including more about public and community health. As more was learned about quality care, it became clear that there were health disparities due in particular to bias, prejudice, and stereotyping. Just as with the issue of quality care, there was a need to monitor disparities, and this led to the development of a monitoring system and report similar to the *National Healthcare Quality and Disparities Report*, which was later combined with the quality report.

Health Professions Education: A Bridge to Quality (2003) This report moved the quality care discussion to health professions education. With the growing recognition that care needed to improve, which required routine monitoring and improvement, it was determined that a key ingredient to accomplishing this objective were the staff—namely, whether they were prepared to provide effective and efficient care to diverse populations. This conclusion and the report were critical in that the recommendations included five core competencies that all healthcare professionals should meet. It is significant that the experts decided to identify competencies that did not focus on one healthcare profession. These competencies are:

1. Provide patient-centered care (person-centered).
2. Work in interprofessional teams.
3. Employ evidence-based practice.
4. Apply quality improvement.
5. Utilize informatics.

Later, the nursing profession developed core competencies for nursing (Quality and Safety Education for nurses [QSEN]) that related to these core health profession competencies; however, it is important that nursing avoids separating itself from these core competencies. The major difference is that QSEN has six competencies and separates quality from safety, and the IOM/NAM recommendation on core competencies considers safety an integral part of quality.

Source: QSEN Institute (2020). *QSEN Institute competencies.* https://qsen.org/competencies/" https://qsen.org/competencies/

Health Literacy (2004) Aimed at examining diversity and disparities, the report *Health Literacy* recognized that health literacy has a major impact on quality care and the health of individuals and communities.

Health Literacy: A Prescription to End Confusion (2004) Communication is critical in healthcare—both written and oral and with all stakeholders. This includes individuals, families, staff, communities, other professionals, and government, among others. Effective partnerships require effective, ongoing communication. When problems with communication occur, health literacy issues may arise. Understanding is necessary for effective healthcare decision-making—affecting locations to obtain treatment, treatment providers, types of treatment, the ability to follow treatment, the ability to engage in self-care, questions to ask healthcare providers, and so on. Yet, millions of Americans cannot understand or act upon this information. This report discussed health literacy and methods to improve communication for individuals and populations.

Keeping Patients Safe: Transforming the Work Environment for Nurses (2004); *The Future of Nursing: Leading Change, Advancing Health* (2010); *The Future of Nursing 2020–2030: Charting a Path to Achieve Health Equity* (2020) Some of the IOM/NAM reports have focused on nursing. One of the significant early reports was *Keeping Patients Safe: Transforming the Work*

Environment for Nurses, which primarily discussed acute care nursing practice, particularly staff nurses and related workforce issues. In 2010, a landmark report titled *The Future of Nursing: Leading Change, Advancing Health* examined current and future roles of nurses. The third report mentioned is directly related to the content of this guide, *The Future of Nursing 2020–2030: Charting a Path to Achieve Health Equity* (2020). These reports are discussed in relevant content in the guide.

The Future of the Public's Health in the 21st Century (2003) and Who Will Keep the Public Healthy? (2003) The initial reports from the IOM focused on acute care, although some of the content could be applied to public and community health. There was slow recognition that separating acute care from public and community health or ignoring the healthcare delivery system as a whole was not effective. In 2003, this view changed with the publication of two key public and community health reports. *The Future of the Public's Health in the 21st Century* examined the need to apply a population health approach, develop effective public health infrastructure, establish partnerships, ensure accountability, implement evidence-based practice, and utilize clear communication. *Who Will Keep the Public Healthy?* turned the focus to identifying the public health competencies, which are related to informatics, genomics, communication, culture, community-based participatory research, global health, policy and law, and public health ethics. The report provided a guide for public and community health education content, such as for nursing.

Informed Consent and Health Literacy (2015) This report discussed a specific issue related to health literacy, which by 2015 was recognized as a major concern in healthcare delivery. Participants in research are asked to sign a consent form, and agreeing to do so should be an informed decision. In order to do this, participants must understand the information they are given. Ensuring that participants can agree and understand prior to participating in a research study is a critical part of ethics and participant rights.

Health Literacy: Past, Present, and Future (2015) Given the concern about health literacy, this report examined the problems, origins, and consequences of adult health literacy. Adults who do not have the required level of health literacy may not be able to engage safely in their own health and healthcare decision-making. The report includes solutions such as the need for organizational changes, including system changes to assist in reducing health literacy.

A Framework for Educating Health Professionals to Address Social Determinants of Health (2016) As more has been learned about the importance of the social determinants of health (SDOH), there has been growing recognition that healthcare professionals need to learn about these determinants so that they are more aware of the impact on health and disparities. From this healthcare, professionals will then be better able to intervene and improve the health of individuals, communities, and populations.

Collaboration Between Health Care and Public Health (2016) This report discussed the need for effective collaboration between acute healthcare and public health. This partnership needs to include shared goals, community engagement, aligned leadership, sustainability, and data and analysis. There are barriers to this collaboration, including inadequate communication, working with interprofessional teams, understanding diverse cultures, and more, that must be addressed.

Communities in Action: Pathways to Health Equity (2017) This report continued to examine health equity, disparities, and SDOH. It particularly noted that we know individual behavior and health status are important, but there is also a need to view these issues from a community perspective. It is the community that has a strong impact on poverty, unemployment, poor education, inadequate housing, poor public transportation, interpersonal violence, and struggling neighborhoods, all of which influence health. Social policies also make a difference in inequalities and contribute to health inequities. The report examined the causes of and possible solutions to health inequities, emphasizing the importance of communities in promoting health equity.

Perspectives on Health Equity and Social Determinants of Health (2017) This report examined the social factors that influence the nation's health (i.e., SDOH); racism and poverty, which result in inequitable social, environmental, and economic conditions; and health disparities. It included content on policies and strategies used to address these problems, focusing on the need for collective actions.

Community-Based Health Literacy Interventions (2018) This report focused on community interventions to reduce health literacy problems, examining types of community-based literacy interventions and methods to evaluate their results. It also provided and described examples. Community infrastructure and staff are critical elements to success, as is a commitment to improve community trust.

Immigration as a Social Determinant of Health (2018) The United States has a large immigrant population, which experiences systematic marginalization and discrimination that often result in health disparities. This report examined the relationship between the immigration experience and health outcomes.

Improving Access to and Equity of Care for People With Serious Illness (2019) At the time this report was completed, the Centers for Disease Control and Prevention estimated that approximately 40 million people in the United States had a serious illness. This type of disease limits daily activities. As health disparities were examined, it was noted that this population also experiences disparities due to race, ethnicity, gender, geography, socioeconomic status, and insurance status. This is found in multiple communities, interfering with healthcare access and quality. Improvement requires engagement and feedback from individuals (patient and family), healthcare providers, organizations, and communities.

Integrating Social Care Into the Delivery of Health Care: Moving Upstream to Improve the Nation's Health (2019) With the recognition of the importance of the SDOH in regards to health equity and disparities, the healthcare delivery system must turn to improvement. The key questions addressed in this report were:

- How can services that address social needs be integrated into clinical care?
- What type of infrastructure will be needed to facilitate that integration?

The report concluded that five complementary activities should be used to ensure integration of social care into health care: awareness, adjustment, assistance, alignment, and advocacy. The report discussed these activities and stated that they should be used by healthcare organizations and providers, communities, social services, and governments.

Population Health in Rural America (2020) Rural areas of the United States experience many health problems and difficulties with receiving effective and timely healthcare. People who live in rural areas are a vulnerable and diverse population. Rural areas also experience serious healthcare delivery problems, such as a shortage of healthcare professionals and services.

Population Health in Challenging Times: Insights From Key Domains: Proceedings of a Workshop (2021) This report examined population health, which is a complex area of healthcare. The workshop identified key areas of concern in population health, supporting the recognition that this type of health is a significant issue in the nation's health.

Priorities on the Health Horizon: Informing PCORI's Strategic Plan (2021) This report discussed the need for more evidence to support healthcare delivery and practice. It particularly focuses on equitable, stakeholder-driven, evidence-guided, patient-centered care. All of this requires effective collaborative relationships between patients, families, clinicians, healthcare administrators, researchers, and policymakers. PCORI is the Patient-Centered Outcomes Research Institute, an independent nonprofit, nongovernmental organization in Washington, DC, that was authorized by Congress in 2010 to address the gap in information needed to make effective healthcare decisions. For more information, visit https://www.pcori.org/about/about-pcori" https://www.pcori.org/about/about-pcori.

Dialogue About the Workforce for Population Health Improvement: Proceedings of a Workshop (2021) This workshop focused on the needs of the population health workforce to improve health. Some of the discussion topics included peer-to-peer chronic disease management educators, health navigators, community health workers, public and health and healthcare leaders, developing competencies of the nonmedical and nonpublic health workforce, and application of the Health in All Policies model.

Exploring the Role of Critical Health Literacy in Addressing the Social Determinants of Health: Proceedings of a Workshop in Brief (2021) Due to the growing concern about the SDOH, a discussion and subsequent report focused on this issue. It particularly addressed the impact of health literacy on SDOH and vulnerable populations. The emphasis was on using literacy strategies to support effective health literacy associated with SDOH.

To Achieve Health Equity, Leverage Nurses and Increase Funding for School and Public Health Nursing (2022) This report focused on nursing, but rather than discussing acute care, it examined the roles of nursing in public health, driven by the need to improve health equity. Improvements in public health nursing education are needed. The key recommendations are for the next 10 years and include:

- Strengthening nursing education
- Promoting diversity, inclusivity, and equity in nursing education and the workforce
- Investing in school and public health nurses

- Protecting nurses' health and well-being
- Preparing nurses for disaster and public health emergency response
- Increasing the number of PhD-prepared nurses

Reducing Inequalities Between Lesbian, Gay, Bisexual, Transgender, and Queer Adolescents and Cisgender, Heterosexual Adolescents: Proceedings of a Workshop (2022) Lesbian, gay, bisexual, transgender, and queer adolescents and cisgender, heterosexual adolescents are at risk for health and social problems. As a vulnerable population, they require assessment and interventions that address health equity and reduce disparities. This report examined these concerns.

Realizing the Promise of Equity in the Organ Transplantation System (2022) Organ transplantation is a complex health need that is supported by a complex system. A key concern is health equities and disparities for some who need this care. This report discussed the many issues patients and families experience and the system that supports organ transplantation.

Closing Evidence Gaps in Clinical Prevention (2022) This report examined the need for more research to provide evidence supporting effective clinical prevention working in collaboration with the U.S. Department of Health and Human Services and U.S. Preventive Services Task Force. For more information, visit https://www.ahrq.gov/cpi/about/otherwebsites/uspstf/index.html.

Examples of Other Reports Related to Health Equity and Disparities

- *Collaboration Between Health Care and Public Health* (2015)
- *The Future of Home Health Care* (2015)
- *Informed Consent and Health Literacy* (2015)
- *Health Literacy: Past, Present, and Future* (2015)
- *Community-Based Health Literacy Interventions* (2018)
- *Improving Access to and Equity of Care for People With Serious Illness* (2019)
- *School Success: An Opportunity for Population Health* (2019)
- *A Roadmap to Reducing Childhood Poverty* (2019)
- *Virtual Clinical Trials: Challenges and Opportunities* (2019)
- *Integrating Social Care Into the Delivery of Health Care: Moving Upstream to Improve the Nation's Health* (2019)

NAM publishes many reports annually. Visit the link below to identify current reports.

Access to IOM/NAM Reports

These reports and other IOM/NAM resources can be read online or downloaded for free using the guest status. Full or parts of reports can be reviewed. There is no fee to access these reports. This information can be accessed at https://nam.edu/publications/.

References

Finkelman, A. (2017). *Teaching the IOM: Implications of the IOM Reports for Nursing Education, Vol. I* (4th ed.). American Nurses Association.

Finkelman, A. (2017). (Vol. 2), *Learning IOM*, adapted content for students and staff. (4th ed.). American Nurses Association.

QSEN Institute (2020). *QSEN Institute competencies*. https://qsen.org/competencies/

Index

A
abuse. *See also* violence
   child, 44–45
addiction, 38. *See also* substance use
   disorders (SUD)
Affordable Care Act (ACA), 27, 52
age-friendly health systems, 21–22
ageism, 23–24. *See also* older adults
alcohol, 38–39, 41. *See also* substance use
   disorders (SUD)
American Academy of Nursing, 34
American Association of Colleges of
   Nursing (AACN), 62
American Hospital Association (AHA), 3
   population health framework, 3–4
American Nurses Association, 47
American Public Health Association
   (APHA), 10

B
Behavioral Risk Factor Surveillance System
   (BRFSS), 38
Biden, J., 35, 36–37
BIPOC (Black, Indigenous, People of Color)
   populations, 2
BRFSS. *See* Behavioral Risk Factor
   Surveillance System (BRFSS)
bullying, 45–46

C
cannabis, 40–41
case management, 7
Centers for Disease Control and Prevention
   (CDC), 4, 47
   Division of Population Health (DPH), 49
   PHHO initiative, 59–60. *See also* Health
     Impact in 5 Years (HI-5)
Centers for Medicare & Medicaid (CMS), 23
child abuse and violence, 44–45
children and teens, 14–19
   common health problems, 17
   COVID-19, 16–17
   health literacy and education, 18

   injury, 16
   LGBTQ+, 24
   mental health problems, 35
   National Survey of Children's Health
     (2019–2020 data), 14–16
   poverty, 18–19
chronic diseases/health problems, 11–12
   diversity, 11
   interventions, 12
   older adults, 20
Commonwealth Fund, 51
Community Health and Economic Prosperity:
   Engaging Businesses as Stewards and
   Stakeholders, 26–27
community services for older adults, 22–23
COVID-19, 2–3, 52
   children and teens, 16–17
   homelessness, 28
   mental health, 33–34
   older adults, 20
   rural health and, 32–33
   socioeconomic status, 27
   SUD and, 41, 42–43

D
disabilities, 14
disease prevention, 54–55
   primary prevention, 54
   secondary prevention, 55
   tertiary prevention, 55
diversity, 9
   chronic diseases/health problems, 11
   rural areas, 32
Division of Population Health (DPH), 49
Domestic Refugee Health Program, 31
drug use, 38–39. *See also* substance use
   disorders (SUD)

E
environmental interventions, 12
ethnic minority populations. *See* racism
evidence-based practice (EBP), 62, 63–64

About the Author

Anita Finkelman is a nurse educator and consultant, currently providing services in the U.S. and Israel, where she has been visiting faculty at Recanati School for Community Health Professions at Ben-Gurion University of the Negev and has consulted with several Israeli universities. She served on the nursing faculty at Bouve College of Health Sciences, School of Nursing, Northeastern University, taught undergraduate and graduate online courses, and led the nursing school's CCNE accreditation process for undergraduate and graduate programs with full accreditation received. Finkelman's past positions include Assistant Professor of Nursing at the University of Oklahoma College of Nursing, undergraduate and graduate nursing online course instructor, and course coordinator for undergraduate nursing research. At the University of Cincinnati, her positions included associate professor/clinical nursing, Director of Continuing Education, and Director of the Undergraduate Program (BSN). She also taught public/community health, mental health nursing, nursing leadership, health policy, and research courses and clinical practicum. She has worked with several smaller colleges to develop and implement online programs and develop curriculum for pre-licensure nursing students.

Finkelman earned her BSN from TCU (Texas) and her master's degree in psychiatric mental health nursing/clinical nurse specialist from Yale University. She completed post-master's graduate work in healthcare policy and administration at George Washington University and participated in the Health Policy Institute, George Mason University as a fellow. Her nursing experience includes clinical, educational, and administrative positions and considerable experience teaching online and developing distance education programs and curriculum. Finkelman has extensive management experience, serving in various positions in psychiatric mental health settings (acute care and community), and has served as Director of Staff Education for two acute care hospitals, as well as in multiple clinical nurse specialist positions. As a consultant, she focuses on the areas of curriculum and quality improvement, teaching-learning practices, distance education, healthcare administration and policy, nursing education accreditation, and assisting nurses in their publishing endeavors.

Finkelman has authored many books, chapters, and journal articles; served on journal editorial boards; and made presentations on nursing education, healthcare administration, health policy, healthcare quality improvement, continuing education, and psychiatric mental health nursing, both nationally and internationally. She also serves as a consultant to publishers in the areas of distance education and product development.

Her current textbooks include: *Professional Nursing Concepts* (Jones and Bartlett Learning, 5th ed., 2021); *Quality Improvement: A Guide for Integration in Nursing*, (Jones & Bartlett Learning, 2nd ed., 2020); *Leadership and Management for Nurses: Core Competencies for Quality Care* (Pearson Education, Inc., 4th ed., 2020); and *Case Management for Nurses* (Pearson Education, Inc., 2010). Additionally, she has published chapters in M. Nies and M. McEwen (Eds.) *Community Health Nursing: Promoting the Health of Aggregates*, Philadelphia, PA: W.B. Saunders Company.

CPSIA information can be obtained
at www.ICGtesting.com
Printed in the USA
LVHW050549060523
746243LV00010B/41